Knitting
California

Knitting California

26 Easy-to-Follow Designs for Beautiful Beanies Inspired by the Golden State

Nancy Bates

To my parents, Romaine and Bernice Machan
Thank you for bringing us to California
and for seeing it for all it could be.

CONTENTS

INTRODUCTION

Welcome to California! From the forests of the North to the deserts of the South, come join my family and me as we share some of our favorite places in the most populous and geologically diverse state in the country. California is, without a doubt, a land of superlatives. The tallest, largest, and oldest trees on earth, the highest and lowest points in the lower forty-eight, and the most national parks (nine in total) are all found within the borders of this unique and beautiful place I call home. Even the mild Mediterranean climate enjoyed by much of the state can only be found in five places in the world. Around here, we're always ready for an adventure! Part travelogue, with a sprinkling of history and personal memoir, this book celebrates not only the amazing natural beauty of the state, but also the cities, the culture, the industries, and even the people—all through the colorful and creative art of knitting.

As soon as the idea of this book became a reality, I sat down with my husband and three grown daughters (all native Californians) to make a list of themes or elements that best represent what we love about our home. Turning these ideas into wearable art and taking family photos along the way truly felt like I was inviting all of you on a knitting road trip! While many designs are uniquely and unmistakably California, such as the State Flag (p. 143), Golden Gate Fog (p. 137), or the palm-tree-lined streets of Los Angeles (p. 23), others were purposely designed to encourage knitters to see in them a bit of their own homes. Sure, monarchs overwinter in California (and Mexico), but they're familiar to everyone. My river in Gold Country (p. 67), has gold at the bottom, but it might remind you of the beloved rivers and trees near your home. And those snow-covered trees of Mammoth Mountain (p. 85) are certainly reminiscent of snowy winters everywhere. The reality is, while some of these elements (mountains, deserts, beaches, etc.) are found in many different locations, having them all together along with Hollywood, thriving citrus and wine industries, classic surf culture, and so much more is what makes California, California! And that is what I'm excited to share with all of you. From cabled trees and bobbled boulders to twisted seaweed, embroidered flowers, and oodles of colorwork, you can now knit your way around the state (no traffic involved), learn some fun facts, and maybe plan to visit someday.

Whether this is your first introduction to California, you've been here before, or you live here like I do, I invite you to sit back, put up your feet, and join me on a knitting tour through my home state. Oh, and don't forget to bring your needles and yarn with you! I'll bring the chips and guacamole!

CHOOSING YARN

All the designs in this book (with the exception of The Lumberjack, pp. 155-159) call for worsted weight yarn—also referred to as a #4. Worsted weight is warm and cozy, making it a great choice for hats. It's also quick and easy to work with (especially when trying new stitches) and doesn't require a lot of yardage per hat. Because it's durable, washable, and has amazing depth of color, I lean toward using Superwash Merino for most designs. Other wools, wool blends, and acrylics are good choices too. Cotton is not recommended due to its lack of memory—the hat will not keep its shape. Whatever you choose, be sure your yarn feels great and has good stitch definition so that all that stitch work isn't lost in the yarn.

Deciding which color yarn to use is one of the exciting parts of starting a new project. YOU get to decide if your hat will be bold and bright, subtle and subdued, or something in between. Many of the hats in this collection were designed to *encourage* personal color choices beyond what I used. Maybe the shape of the California Poppies (pp. 97–101) reminds you of a particular pink flower you adore. Go ahead and switch it up! Are the sunsets *your* favorite part of Los Angeles (pp. 23–27)? Imagine that cityscape knitted against an orange sky. The plaid of The Lumberjack (p. 155) and the checkerboard design of The Central Valley (p. 73) are perfect for just about any color combo. And Mammoth Mountain (p. 85)? Red, orange, green, purple? Go for it! The color choices are endless! Raid your stash. Try something new. It's all up to you. If you're familiar with *Knitting the National Parks*, you might recognize many of the same yarns and colors used here as well. I'm a huge fan of stash busting!

GAUGE AND SIZING

Achieving the correct gauge (number of stitches per 1 in. / 2.5 cm) in your knitting is very important in making sure your hat fits. If you knit too tightly, your hat will be small; too loosely, and it will be large. The hats in this book are designed to be "one size fits most adults." They will fit if you have the correct gauge. Before beginning your chosen design, knit a small swatch (about 4 in. / 10 cm square) in stockinette stitch (or other stitch as specified in the pattern) with the same yarn and same needle you plan to use for the hat. You can also use a "gauge in the round" method if you prefer. Block the swatch, let dry, and then carefully count your stitches against a ruler. Adjust your needles as needed until you get the correct gauge. If you want your hat to fit bigger or smaller, simply go up or down one or two needle sizes to achieve the desired fit. You can also make your hat a bit "slouchier" by adding rows or a bit shorter by removing rows. This takes some thought and planning to be sure your addition or subtraction of rows doesn't interfere with the design. When possible, make these optional changes in areas such as plain stockinette stitch sections.

CASTING ON

When choosing a cast-on method, be sure to choose one that is stretchy and suitable for hats. The long-tail cast-on is my preferred method and the one I use throughout this book. It's consistent, simple, neat, and flexible. If you want to experiment with another method, test a sample ribbing first to check for flexibility before continuing with your hat.

WET BLOCKING A HAT

Wet blocking is a technique used to give knitted items a neater, finished appearance. It's especially important in stranded colorwork beacuse it helps relax the stitches and even out the tension. It also rounds out the top of a hat to reduce any unwanted pointiness. It can even help a hat that's slightly too tight fit a little better.

1. Begin by soaking the hat in a small tub or bowl of cool water. Add a little no-rinse wool wash to the water if desired. If you're concerned about color transfer between dark and light colors, add a commercial "color catching" sheet to the water. Attach the ribbing end of the hat to the side of the tub using a large clip, keeping the ribbing just above the water level while the rest of the hat soaks. Leaving the ribbing above the waterline keeps it from stretching out too much. Soak the hat for a few minutes.

2. Carefully lift the hat from the water, supporting it from the bottom to avoid excess stretching. Keep the ribbing toward the top to keep it dry, then gently squeeze out as much water as possible from the hat. Do NOT wring or twist.

3. Roll the hat in a clean, dry towel and gently, but firmly, press down on the towel to remove excess water.

4. Carefully place your hat across an overturned bowl or other rounded object (even a balloon) to dry. Be sure the object is the size you want your finished hat to be. Smooth out any uneven stitches and very gently pull or stretch the hat as needed to remove puckers or make the hat a little bigger. Pat down and shape the crown of the hat, removing any unwanted pointiness. Allow the hat to dry overnight.

SOUTHERN
CALIFORNIA

Anza Borrego Blooms

Anza Borrego Desert State Park (the largest state park in California) is filled with all sorts of adventure opportunities from camping and hiking to horseback riding and golf, but is probably most famous for three special features—wildflowers, metal sculptures, and dark skies. People don't often think of deserts and blooms as going together. But, for Anza Borrego Desert, the eagerly anticipated blooming season in spring is one of its biggest draws for visitors. Wildflower viewing is *so* popular that a Wildflower Hotline has been set up through the park's website for up-to-date information on what's blooming and where to see it. Through careful monitoring of rainfall, temperature, and other factors, experts

can usually predict whether there *will* be a "super bloom," but they can't predict precisely *when* it will happen. That part is a bit of a mystery. Even without a "super bloom," the sporadic patches of colorful wildflowers scattered throughout the park each spring are spectacular. You'll find them out in the open among ocotillo cactus or tucked away in unexpected places as you explore the park. We once saw a tiny patch of pink flowers blooming right next to The Slot, our favorite little (but adventurous) slot canyon trail. For an extra treat, stay until day's end—the colors of the flowers almost seem to glow in the golden light just before sunset.

What about those metal sculptures? In and around the tiny town of Borrego Springs (the jumping-off point to the state park) you'll find about 130 amazing life-size and bigger-than-life-size metal sculptures of dinosaurs, birds, people, and even a dragon. Created by artist Ricardo Breceda, these extremely detailed and very impressive examples of outdoor art can be found throughout the landscape. Picking up a map and stopping to see as many as you can is like a giant outdoor scavenger hunt. Each one draws you in for a closer look. A selfie with a life-size T-Rex? Yes, please!

Wildflowers and sculptures aside, the incredible dark skies and stargazing opportunities are reason enough to make Anza Borrego Desert a weekend or vacation destination. With more than three hundred good stargazing nights a year, you can find amateur and professional astronomers out with their telescopes year-round. There's nothing quite like an evening spent gazing up at the stars, planets, and galaxies to remind us how amazing the universe is.

This easy-to-knit stranded colorwork design was inspired by patches of wildflowers against the neutral backdrop of the desert floor. Three different colors and three slightly different stitch patterns create a colorful landscape reminiscent of a springtime "super bloom."

SIZE

One size fits an average adult size head (approx. 19 in. / 48 cm to 22 in. / 56 cm). Finished Circumference: approx. 20¼ in. / 51.5 cm.

YARN

Worsted weight yarn (#4) in five colors. Shown in:

- ☐ **A:** Stunning String Studio Legacy Worsted: Biscotti (25 g / 54 yd. / 49 m)
- ▨ **B:** Aly Bee Workshop Merino Worsted: Prickly Pear (25 g / 50 yd. / 46 m)
- ☐ **C:** Stunning String Studio Legacy Worsted: Fading Sunlight (10 g / 22 yd. / 20 m)
- ■ **D:** Polka Dot Sheep Whitefish Worsted: Huckleberry (10 g / 22 yd. / 20 m)
- ▨ **E:** Malabrigo Rios: English Rose (10 g / 21 yd. / 20 m)

NEEDLES

- US size 5 / 3.75 mm, 16 in. / 40 cm circular knitting needles
- US size 7 / 4.5 mm, 16 in. (40 cm) circular knitting needles
- US size 7 / 4.5 mm set of double-pointed needles (DPNs) (or size needed to obtain gauge)

Continued on next page

NOTIONS

- 3 stitch markers (two of one color and one of another color)
- Tapestry needle for weaving in ends

GAUGE

With larger needles, approx. 9½ stitches = 2 in. / 5 cm in stranded stockinette stitch blocked.

Note: If you already know you are a tight knitter (or just want a larger hat), go up one or two needle sizes for both the ribbing and the body of the hat.

KNITTING INSTRUCTIONS

With smaller circular needles and color A, cast on 96 stitches. Place single color marker and join in the round, being careful not to twist stitches.

Work (k1, p1) ribbing pattern for 1½ to 2 in. / 4 to 5 cm.

Switch to larger needles and work chart from right to left beginning on Row 1, bottom right corner. Chart repeats three times around the hat. Use remaining two stitch markers of another color to mark chart repeats.

Note: In order to avoid long "floats" (strands of yarn on the inside of the hat) and to help maintain your tension, do not carry a color more than three or four stitches without twisting the colors around each other in the back of work.

Switch to DPNs when work becomes too small for circular needles.

FINISHING

After chart is complete, cut yarn, leaving a 10 in. / 25.5 cm tail. Using a tapestry needle, weave tail through remaining stitches and pull tightly to close circle. Pull tail to inside and weave in all ends.

Block as desired. See p. 12 for my favorite hat blocking technique.

KEY

▢	A
▢	B
▢	C
▢	D
▢	E
▢	K Knit
◩	K2tog Knit 2 together
⋁	S1 Slip 1 purl-wise with yarn in back
◼	No stitch

Note: The "no stitch" squares are placeholders for stitches that are gained or lost throughout the design. *Do not skip a stitch.* Simply treat these squares as if they do not exist.

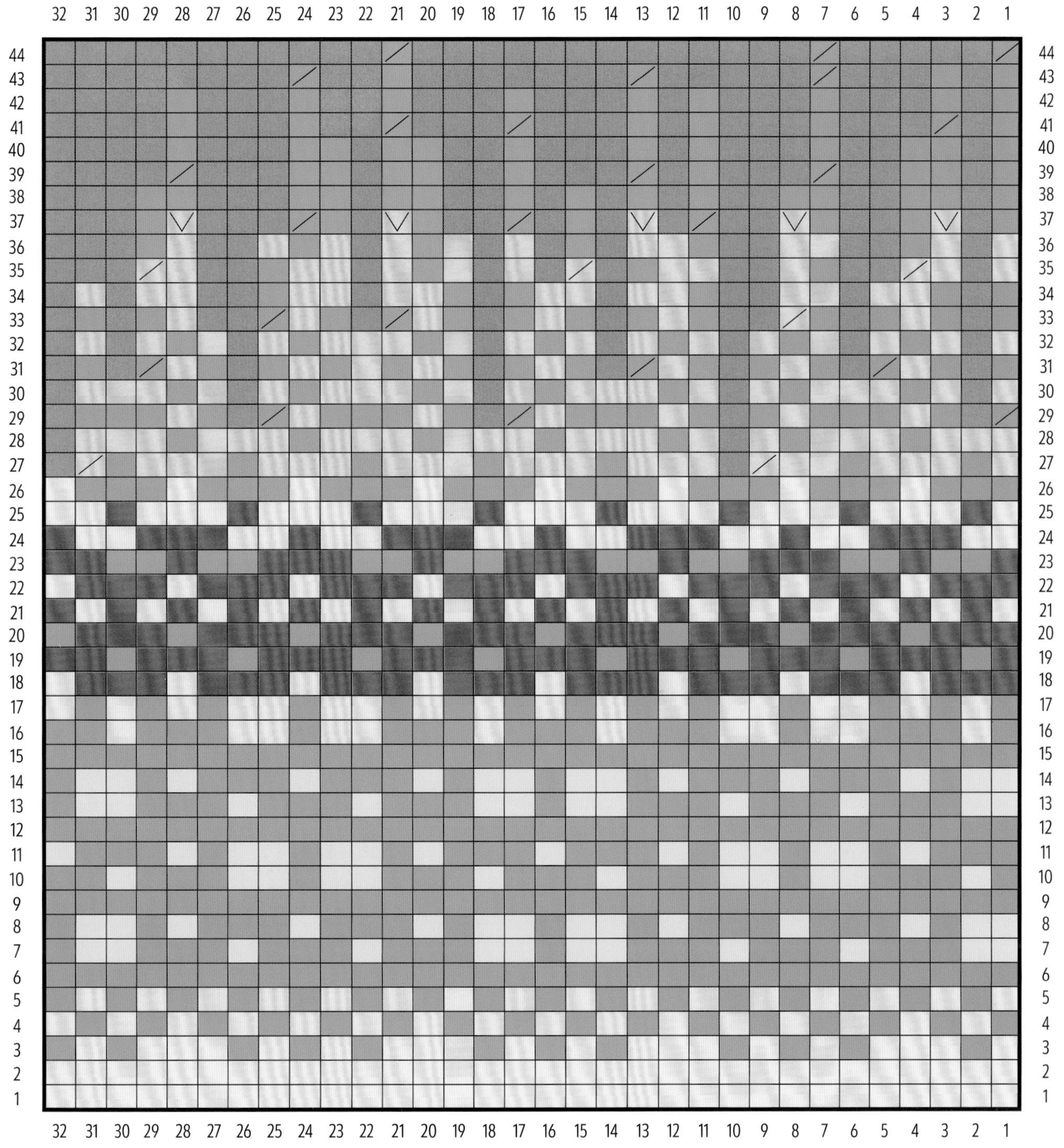
32 31 30 29 28 27 26 25 24 23 22 21 20 19 18 17 16 15 14 13 12 11 10 9 8 7 6 5 4 3 2 1
44 43 42 41 40 39 38 37 36 35 34 33 32 31 30 29 28 27 26 25 24 23 22 21 20 19 18 17 16 15 14 13 12 11 10 9 8 7 6 5 4 3 2 1

Los Angeles

I'm not really a city person. In fact, I usually avoid them. When we travel, we stay in cities long enough to fly in, rent a car, and drive out. Even so, I understand why some people love them. Perhaps it's that each city has its own "personality" and unique characteristics that make it feel like home. When I think of particular cities, certain images come to mind. Chicago? I think of baseball and wind. New York? Broadway plays and crowded sidewalks. Boston? History and marathons. These images may not be exactly what makes these cities unique, but as an outsider, this is what I think of. Only the people who live there can truly describe what makes them special. What comes to mind when *you* think of Los Angeles?

Palm trees, traffic, nature, entertainment? All would be correct. But, in the spirit of sharing my home state with you, here's *my* list of fun facts and personal opinions about what makes L.A. unique.

Although it sounds incredibly cliché, the general "vibe" of L.A. really is laid-back, more casual and less business-like than some other cities. Sure, many of our freeways are *very* congested, but (contrary to what movies or TV would have you believe) nobody sits in traffic and honks their horn. It just doesn't help. Most people in L.A. describe distance in time, not miles. How far is it to the theater? About forty minutes. It's silly, but it makes sense. On the other hand, I have no explanation for why we put "the" in front of highway or freeway numbers while talking about them. "Take the 15 north to the 10 east!"

As far as cities go, the cluster of skyscrapers in L.A. is rather small, which is a good thing considering the proximity to earthquake faults. What L.A. lacks in height of skyscapers, it makes up for in urban and suburban sprawl. The city goes on for miles and miles in almost every direction. Many first-time visitors are surprised by the proximity of L.A. to nature, reaching from the rugged San Gabriel mountains all the way to the coast. This closeness to nature and the sunny weather makes outdoor activities very popular. Within ninety minutes or less from L.A., you can be skiing in the mountains, surfing at the beach, or rock climbing and hiking in the desert. One of my favorite L.A. experiences? Shopping in the huge fabric district with the scent of L.A. Street Dogs in the air—sizzling bacon-wrapped hot dogs topped with sautéed onions and peppers.

This design was inspired by perhaps one of the most iconic images of Los Angeles: palm trees. They are truly everywhere, from the beach to the foothills and in every suburb in every direction, even in the heart of L.A. with the city skyline in the background, just like on this fun-to-knit beanie.

SIZE

One size fits an average adult size head (approx. 19 in. / 48 cm to 22 in. / 56 cm). Finished circumference: approx. 20¼ in. / 51.5 cm.

YARN

Worsted weight yarn (#4) in five colors. Shown in:

- **A:** Polka Dot Sheep Whitefish Worsted: Barnwood (25 g / 55 yd. / 50 m)
- **B:** Malabrigo, Rios: Camel (10 g / 22 yd. / 20 m)
- **C:** Peekaboo Yarns Merino Worsted: Classic Silver (20 g / 44 yd. / 40 m)
- **D:** Malabrigo, Rios: Ivy (10 g / 22 yd. / 20 m)
- **E:** Stunning String Studio Merino Worsted: Big Sky (20 g / 43 yd. / 39 m)

NEEDLES

- US size 5 / 3.75 mm, 16 in. / 40 cm circular knitting needles
- US size 7 / 4.5 mm, 16 in. / 40 cm circular knitting needles
- US size 7 / 4.5 mm set of double-pointed needles (DPNs) (or size needed to obtain gauge)

Continued on next page

NOTIONS

- 3 stitch markers (two of one color and one of another color)
- Tapestry needle for weaving in ends and working duplicate stitches

GAUGE

With larger needles, approx. 9½ stitches = 2 in. / 5 cm in stranded stockinette stitch blocked.

Note: If you already know you are a tight knitter (or just want a larger hat), go up one or two needle sizes for both the ribbing and the body of the hat.

KNITTING INSTRUCTIONS

With smaller circular needles and color A, cast on 96 stitches. Place single color marker and join in the round, being careful not to twist stitches.

Work (k1, p1) ribbing pattern for 1½ to 2 in. / 4 to 5 cm.

Switch to larger needles and work chart from right to left beginning on Row 1, bottom right corner. Chart repeats three times around the hat. Use remaining two stitch markers of another color to mark chart repeats.

Note: In order to avoid long "floats" (strands of yarn on the inside of the hat) and to help maintain your tension, do not carry a color more than three or four stitches without twisting the colors around each other in the back of work.

Switch to DPNs when work becomes too small for circular needles.

FINISHING

After chart is complete, cut yarn, leaving a 10 in. / 25.5 cm tail. Using a tapestry needle, weave tail through remaining stitches and pull tightly to close circle. Pull tail to inside and weave in all ends.

Block as desired. See p.12 for my favorite hat blocking technique.

Work duplicate stitches where shown to fill in the tree trunks.

KEY

■	A
■	B
□	C
■	D
■	E
□	K Knit
D	Duplicate Stitch To be done after all other knitting is complete
V	S1 Slip 1 purl-wise with yarn in back
/	K2tog Knit 2 together
■	No stitch **Note:** The "no stitch" squares are placeholders for stitches that are gained or lost throughout the design. *Do not skip a stitch.* Simply treat these squares as if they do not exist.

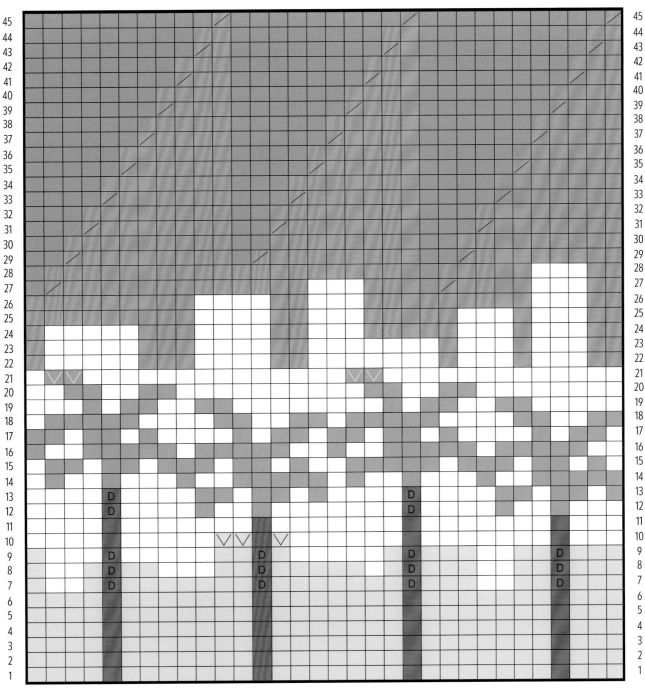

SoCal Surf

Ahhhhh ... the iconic images of surfing in Southern California: waves, sand, woody wagons, bikinis, surfboards, wetsuits, bonfires, parties on the beach, and palm trees. It all sounds like classic SoCal surf. But these images actually represent two distinct views of surfing. The first is the more "reality-based" side of surfing—skill, practice, sports, and competitions. The other side is more "fantasy-based"—think Frankie and Annette movies and the Beach Boys. Whichever way *you* look at SoCal surf culture, it's certain to include fun and sun!

The history of surfing goes back hundreds of years, originating in Hawaii and other Polynesian islands. It wasn't until the early 1900s that surfing came to the mainland. After a demonstration at Huntington Beach, California, in 1910, word of this new sport began to spread and in

1959, the first West Coast Surfing Championship was held, also in Huntington Beach, now known as "Surf City USA." It was right about this time that the popularity of the sport itself and the perceived carefree lifestyle of surfers sparked an interest in surf/beach culture that spread nationwide. A wave of California beach party movies hit the theaters, complete with bikini-clad dancers and surfing shenanigans. Around this same time, a group of brothers and friends formed a band in Hawthorne, California, and called themselves the Beach Boys. Although only one of the band members actually surfed, the songs of the Beach Boys celebrated everything that everyone loved about surf culture. I remember going to a Beach Boys concert in high school with my boyfriend in the '70s. I embroidered flowers on my cut-off jeans and sewed matching Hawaiian shirts for us to wear. So perfectly California! It was a time when it seemed everyone thought if you were from California, you knew how to surf. When my family visited relatives in eastern Canada when

I was a teenager, one of the first things my cousin asked was, "Why don't you have a tan?"

Although the silly beach party movies are a thing of the past, they will always represent the era of surf scene–turned–pop culture. The music of the Beach Boys (some of the best songs ever written) is still popular today and will forever spark feelings of nostalgia. Surfing itself has grown into a multimillion-dollar industry, encompassing surf equipment and gear, surf-inspired clothing, and surfing competitions around the world.

This classic striped beanie design was inspired by the surf culture of the '50s and '60s, when young surfers piled their friends and their boards into a woody wagon and headed to the beach. Following a ribbing in the color of sand, a rectangular pattern like the panels of a woody wagon comes next. Various widths of stripes inspired by the desaturated colors of vintage surfboards complete the look.

SIZE

One size fits an average adult size head (approx. 19 in. / 48 cm to 22 in. / 56 cm). Finished circumference: approx. 20¼ in. / 51.5 cm.

YARN

Worsted weight yarn (#4) in eight colors. Shown in:

Ribbing color (not shown on chart): Aly Bee Workshop: Sandcastle (17g/ 34yd/ 30m)

☐ **A:** Aly Bee Workshop Merino Worsted: Lemonade (10 g / 20 yd. / 18 m)

■ **B:** Stunning String Studio Legacy Worsted: Rusty Gate (12 g / 26 yd. / 24 m)

☐ **C:** Aly Bee Workshop Merino Worsted: Sea Spray (10 g / 20 yd. / 18 m)

☐ **D:** Aly Bee Workshop Merino Worsted: Blush (10 g / 20 yd. / 18 m)

☐ **E:** Aly Bee Workshop Merino Worsted: Honeybee (10 g / 20 yd. / 18 m)

■ **F:** Aly Bee Workshop Merino Worsted: Nectarine (10 g / 20 yd. / 18 m)

☐ **G:** Aly Bee Workshop Merino Worsted: Kettle Corn (5 g / 10 yd. / 9 m)

■ **H:** Aly Bee Workshop Merino Worsted: Gaia (10 g / 20 yd. / 18 m)

Continued on next page

NEEDLES

- US size 5 / 3.75 mm, 16 in. / 40 cm circular knitting needles
- US size 7 / 4.5 mm, 16 in. / 40 cm circular knitting needles

US size 7 / 4.5 mm set of double-pointed needles (DPNs) (or size needed to obtain gauge)

NOTIONS

- 3 stitch markers (two of one color and one of another color)
- Tapestry needle for weaving in ends

GAUGE

With larger needles, approx. 9½ stitches = 2 in. / 5 cm in stranded stockinette blocked.

Note: If you already know you are a tight knitter (or just want a larger hat), go up one or two needle sizes for both the ribbing and the body of the hat.

KNITTING INSTRUCTIONS

With smaller circular needles and ribbing color, cast on 96 stitches. Place single color marker and join in the round, being careful not to twist stitches.

Work (k1, p1) ribbing pattern for 1½ to 2 in. / 4 to 5 cm.

Switch to larger needles and work chart from right to left beginning on Row 1, bottom right corner. Chart repeats three times around the hat. Use remaining two stitch markers of another color to mark chart repeats.

Note: In order to avoid long "floats" (strands of yarn on the inside of the hat) and to help maintain your tension, do not carry a color more than three or four stitches without twisting the colors around each other in the back of work.

Switch to DPNs when work becomes too small for circular needles.

FINISHING

After chart is complete, cut yarn, leaving a 10 in. / 25.5 cm tail. Using a tapestry needle, weave tail through remaining stitches and pull tightly to close circle. Pull tail to inside and weave in all ends.

Block as desired. See p. 12 for my favorite hat blocking technique.

KEY

⬜	A
⬛	B
🟦	C
🟦	D
⬜	E
⬛	F
⬜	G
🟦	H
⬜	K — Knit
◩	K2tog — Knit 2 together
⬛	No stitch

Note: The "no stitch" squares are placeholders for stitches that are gained or lost throughout the design. *Do not skip a stitch.* Simply treat these squares as if they do not exist.

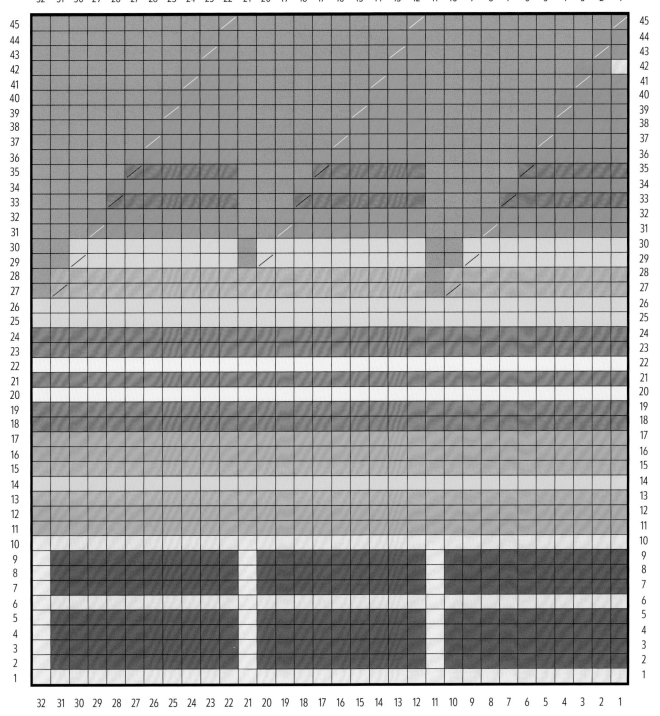

Los Colores de México
(The Colors of Mexico)

With hundreds of Spanish-named cities, streets, and beaches, from San Diego to San Francisco (and beyond), it's clear to see that Spanish and Mexican roots run deep in California, especially in the south. This heritage is a huge part of who we are as a state and of anyone who lives here. Even without realizing it, the influence is all around us, from the architecture of famous buildings and ordinary homes to the colors and patterns of pottery, tiles, and textiles. We're drawn to historic (or historically recreated) places like Olvera Street in Los Angeles or Old Town, San Diego. Ballet Folklórico dances are part of almost every festival,

we learn Mexican folk songs in school, and most of us have taken a swing at many a candy-filled piñata at birthday parties or family picnics.

Then, of course, there's the food. Growing up in Southern California, Mexican food was just as much a part of our lives as hamburgers, spaghetti, Chinese food, and meatloaf. I figured it was that way for everybody. I found out otherwise when my grandma came to visit from Canada in the late 1960s when I was about eight or nine. Just the two of us were home one day, so I rode my bike to the local taco place to pick up some tacos for lunch. A bit hesitant at first, Grandma was a huge fan after only a couple bites. Over the next few days, she kept sending me back for more tacos! Lucky for all of us, Mexican restaurants can now be found almost everywhere! Aside from the delicious food, most Mexican restaurants have another thing in common—the beautiful colors of Mexico!

A gentle nod to the Mexican heritage of California, this fun and colorful design was inspired by the beautiful embroidery found on peasant-style blouses and Ballet Folklórico dresses. I am a *huge* fan of embroidery, especially the embroidery found on the clothing of many cultures around the world. Knowing that each stitch, image, and color choice reflects the life and culture of the person who stitched it is fascinating. And it's so beautiful! This beanie features colorful images of birds and flowers against a solid base with the addition of embroidered French knots and simple straight stitches to add even more dimension and pops of color. Begin with a base color of your choice (natural, black, pink, blue, etc.) and then adjust the colors of the images to create your own unique design. Whatever colors you choose, you'll be bringing the colors of Mexico to life.

SIZE

One size fits an average adult size head (approx. 19 in. / 48 cm to 22 in. / 56 cm). Finished circumference: approx. 20¼ in. / 51.5 cm.

YARN

Worsted weight yarn (#4) in nine colors. Shown in (main photo):

☐ **A:** Malabrigo, Rios: Natural (50 g / 105 yd. / 96 m)

Approx. (3 g / 6 yd. / 5 m) to (10 g / 20 yd. / 18 m) each of the following colors:

■ **B:** Peekaboo Yarns Merino Worsted: Biscayne Blue

☐ **C:** Peekaboo Yarns Merino Worsted: Orange Blaze

■ **D:** Aly Bee Workshop Merino Worsted: Festive

☐ **E:** Aly Bee Workshop Merino Worsted: Costa del Sol

☐ **F:** Stunning String Studio Legacy Worsted: Pasture

☐ **G:** Stunning String Studio Legacy Worsted: Field Flowers

☐ **H:** Stunning String Studio Legacy Worsted: Goldenrod

■ **I:** Stunning String Studio Legacy Worsted: Little Black Dress

Note: I used natural for the main color (color A) and an assortment of eight other colors for the knitted motifs and embroidered accents. This design would also look great using black, pink, yellow, or blue for the main color. Have fun making it just like mine or an entirely different color arrangement. The possibilities are endless! It's a great design for using up bits of leftover colors.

Continued on next page

NEEDLES

- US size 5 / 3.75 mm, 16 in. / 40 cm circular knitting needles
- US size 7 / 4.5 mm, 16 in. / 40 cm circular knitting needles
- US size 7 / 4.5 mm set of double-pointed needles (DPNs) (or size needed to obtain gauge)

NOTIONS

- 3 stitch markers (two of one color and one of another color)
- Tapestry needle for weaving in ends and working duplicate stitches and embroidery

GAUGE

With larger needles, approx. 9½ stitches = 2 in. / 5 cm in stranded stockinette stitch blocked.

Note: If you already know you are a tight knitter (or just want a larger hat), go up one or two needle sizes for both the ribbing and the body of the hat.

KNITTING INSTRUCTIONS

With smaller circular needles and color A, cast on 96 stitches. Place single color marker and join in the round, being careful not to twist stitches.

Work (k1, p1) ribbing pattern for 1½ to 2 in. / 4 to 5 cm.

Switch to larger needles and work chart from right to left beginning on Row 1, bottom

right corner. Chart repeats three times around the hat. Use remaining two stitch markers of another color to mark chart repeats.

Note: In order to avoid long "floats" (strands of yarn on the inside of the hat) and to help maintain your tension, do not carry a color more than three or four stitches without twisting the colors around each other in the back of work.

Switch to DPNs when work becomes too small for circular needles.

FINISHING

After chart is complete, cut yarn, leaving a 10 in. / 25.5 cm tail. Using a tapestry needle, weave tail through remaining stitches and pull tightly to close circle. Pull tail to inside and weave in all ends.

Block as desired. See p. 12 for my favorite hat blocking technique.

Embroidery: After all blocking is complete, add duplicate stitches where shown.

Using photos as a guide, work the rest of the embroidery. I used French knots for the eyes of the birds (single wrap for small birds, double wrap for large birds) and the centers of some of the flowers. Use assorted lengths of straight stitches for the leaves of the smaller flowers, the centers of the larger flowers, and the beaks and wings of the birds. Have fun experimenting with different colors and stitches.

KEY

☐	A
■	B
☐	C
■	D
☐	E
☐	F
☐	G
☐	H
■	I
☐	K Knit
F	French knots (see p. 185) to be worked after all other knitting is complete. In the meantime, knit with base color.
D	Duplicate Stitch To be done after all other knitting is complete
╱	K2tog Knit 2 together
▨	No stitch **Note:** The "no stitch" squares are placeholders for stitches that are gained or lost throughout the design. *Do not skip a stitch.* Simply treat these squares as if they do not exist.

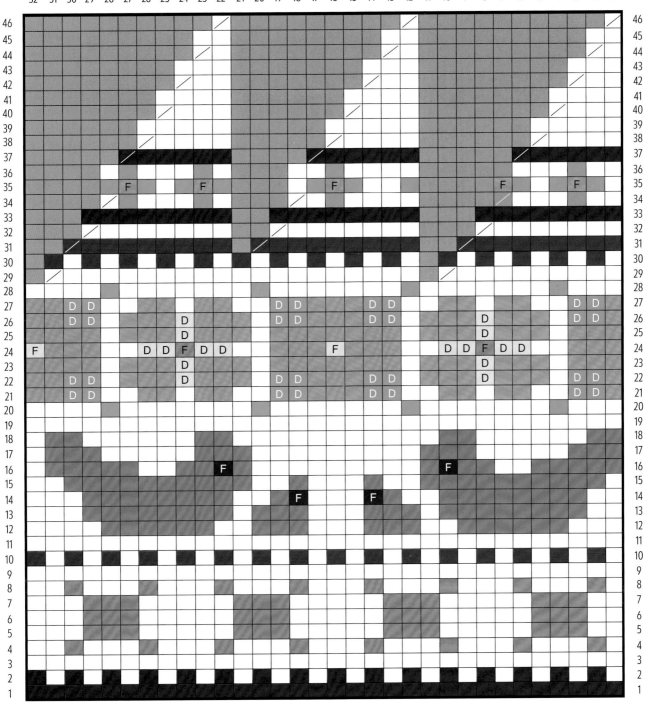

Mojave Desert

One of the most intriguing aspects of desert landscapes is the secrets they seem to hide, visible only to those who take the time to look. The drive from L.A. to Las Vegas along "the 15" includes about a two-hour stretch through the Mojave Desert, known to locals as "the high desert" due to its elevation. Many travelers see this as a place to get through as quickly as possible. Because the Mojave covers such a huge section of the southeastern corner of the state (including portions of Joshua Tree and Death Valley National Parks), getting through it quickly really isn't an option. A better idea? Discover its secrets and see it for its beauty. Even better, take a few days to do it.

From the highway, mountains with jagged peaks or gradual slopes and even ancient volcanic cinder cones can be seen in the distance in almost every direction. This alone makes for a beautiful backdrop for a road trip, especially in early morning or late afternoon sun. For a *closer* look at what the Mojave has to offer, paved and unpaved roads off the main highways lead to sand dunes, ghost towns, salt flats, a lava tube, and so much more. With location names such as Castle Mountains, Devils Playground, or Trilobite Wilderness, who can resist a little side trip? No matter where you travel in the Mojave, the sunsets will be spectacular. Be sure to look up after dark for some incredible dark-sky stargazing. Almost every time we pass through the Mojave Desert at night, we pull off onto a side road just to stop and gaze at the stars for a bit.

Perhaps the most hidden secrets of the desert are the flora and fauna. The animals of the Mojave range from cougars, bighorn sheep, and coyotes to lizards, snakes, tortoises, and tiny mice. Since most stay hidden from humans, spotting them in the wild is a rare treat, though I have seen some very colorful lizards! Plant life ranges from creosote bushes and Joshua trees to juniper and pinyon pine. Perhaps the most hidden treasures of all are the various species of cactus, especially beautiful when they're in bloom.

In sun-washed colors of the desert, this design features colorful striped bands with rows of prickly pear and barrel cactus. Leave the finished design as is, or, for additional texture and color, add needles and blooms to the cactus using simple embroidered straight stitches and French knots.

SIZE

One size fits an average adult size head (approx. 19 in. / 48 cm to 22 in. / 56 cm). Finished circumference: approx. 20¼ in. / 51.5 cm.

YARN

Worsted weight yarn (#4) in four to six colors. Shown in:

- ☐ **A:** Manos Del Uruguay, Alegria Grande: Malaquita (25 g / 55 yd. / 50 m)
- ☐ **B:** Aly Bee Workshop Merino Worsted: Prickly Pear (25 g / 50 yd. / 46 m)
- ☐ **C:** Malabrigo, Rios: Frank Ochre (25 g / 53 yd. / 48 m)
- ☐ **D:** Malabrigo, Rios: Ivory (25 g / 53 yd. / 48 m)

Optional: About 3 g / 6 yd. / 5 m each of any pink or yellow worsted weight (#4) yarn for embroidered blooms on the cactus.

NEEDLES

- US size 5 / 3.75 mm, 16 in. / 40 cm circular knitting needles
- US size 7 / 4.5 mm, 16 in. / 40 cm circular knitting needles
- US size 7 / 4.5 mm set of double-pointed needles (DPNs) (or size needed to obtain gauge)

Continued on next page

NOTIONS

- 3 stitch markers (two of one color and one of another color)
- Tapestry needle for weaving in ends and working optional embroidery

GAUGE

With larger needles, approx. 9½ stitches = 2 in. / 5 cm in stranded stockinette stitch blocked.

Note: If you already know you are a tight knitter (or just want a larger hat), go up one or two needle sizes for both the ribbing and the body of the hat.

KNITTING INSTRUCTIONS

With smaller circular needles and color A, cast on 96 stitches. Place single color marker and join in the round, being careful not to twist stitches.

Work (k2, p2) ribbing pattern for 1½ to 2 in. / 4 to 5 cm.

Switch to larger needles and work chart from right to left beginning on Row 1, bottom right corner. Chart repeats three times around the hat. Use remaining two stitch markers of another color to mark chart repeats.

Note: In order to avoid long "floats" (strands of yarn on the inside of the hat) and to help maintain your tension,

do not carry a color more than three or four stitches without twisting the colors around each other in the back of work.

FINISHING

After chart is complete, cut yarn, leaving a 10 in. / 25.5 cm tail. Using a tapestry needle, weave tail through remaining stitches and pull tightly to close circle. Pull tail to inside and weave in all ends.

Block as desired. See p. 12 for my favorite hat blocking technique.

Optional Embroidery: After all blocking is complete, add needles and blooms to the prickly pear cactus using simple straight stitches. Using photos as a guide, add as many or as few as you'd like. I used color D (Ivory) for the cactus needles. Add blooms to the barrel cactus using French knots (see p. 185).

KEY

▢	A
▢	B
▢	C
▢	D
▢	K Knit
◩	K2tog Knit 2 together
◼	No stitch

Note: The "no stitch" squares are placeholders for stitches that are gained or lost throughout the design. *Do not skip a stitch.* Simply treat these squares as if they do not exist.

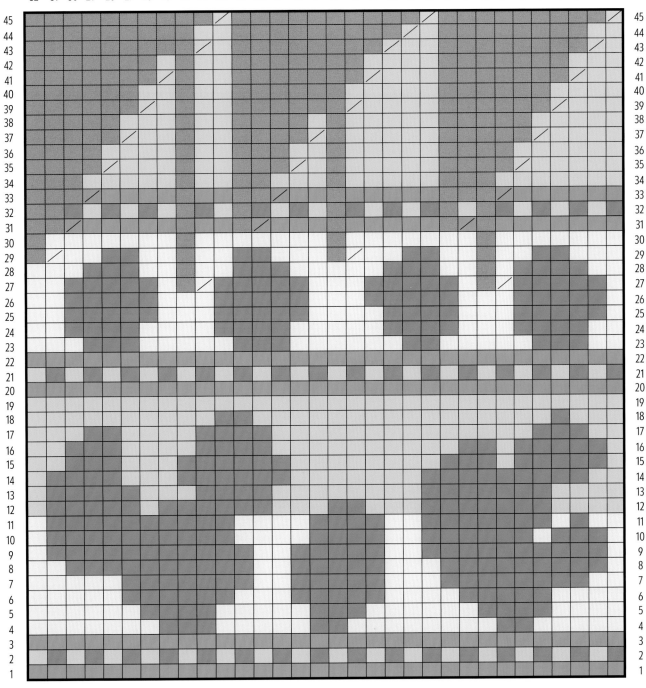

Hollywood

Lights! Camera! Action! Three little words that immediately conjure up images of the glitz and glamour of classic Hollywood moviemaking. Makeup gets a touch-up, actors take their places, the director sits in a canvas chair, and then—Action! The magic begins. Today's call-outs: Roll Sound! Speeding! Background! or Marker! may not sound as simplistically classic, but they still end in "Action!"—and the magic begins. Movies have transported us to faraway places, different times, and other worlds since their humble beginnings of short silent films in the late 1800s. As the industry grew, moviemakers headed to California, lured by consistently milder weather and lots of sunshine. The Golden Age of Hollywood cinema began. By the 1920s and '30s, with several major movie studios in production at once, Hollywood was considered the movie capital of the world.

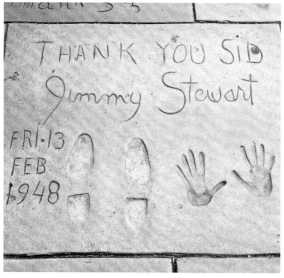

Today, although many of the original studios have turned to television and there are major movie studios around the world, Hollywood (Tinseltown) still holds that image of being all about movies, celebrities, entertainment, and glamour. After all, can you really mention the name *Hollywood* and *not* think of movies?

For movie fans worldwide, a visit to California must include a trip to Tinseltown. Finding your favorite stars on the iconic Walk of Fame is classic Hollywood, as is a stop at Mann's Chinese Theatre, where the handprints and footprints of celebrities are preserved in concrete. You just *have* to compare your own hand to theirs. Spoiler alert! A lot of them seem really small. We once happened to be in Hollywood the day before a big awards ceremony at Mann's Chinese Theatre. They actually set up a red carpet! So classic. The famous Hollywood Bowl, built in 1922, is still an amazing concert setting. If you happen to be in town at the right time, a movie-under-the-stars experience on the lawn of Hollywood Forever Cemetery is a treat. And don't forget to snap a photo of one of the most famous images of Hollywood—the Hollywood sign.

Inspired by the classic moviemaking images of a film strip and clapperboard, this black and white design is easy to knit. Add a bit of Tinseltown flair with a pop-pom made of black and gold yarns held together. The black ties in with the design and the gold is reminiscent of a golden Oscar award.

SIZE

One size fits an average adult size head (approx. 19 in. / 48 cm to 22 in. / 56 cm) Finished circumference: approx. 20¼ in. / 51.5 cm.

YARN

Worsted weight yarn (#4) in two colors. Shown in:

- ■ **A:** Stunning String Studio, Legacy Worsted: Little Black Dress (60 g / 129 yd. / 118 m)
- ☐ **B:** Malabrigo, Rios: Natural (25 g / 53 yd. / 49 m)

NEEDLES

- US size 5 / 3.75 mm, 16 in. / 40 cm circular knitting needles
- US size 7 / 4.5 mm, 16 in. / 40 cm circular knitting needles
- US size 7 / 4.5 mm set of double-pointed needles (DPNs) (or size needed to obtain gauge)

Continued on next page

The Citrus Industry

Citrus and sunshine go together like, well, citrus and sunshine! Not only are oranges, lemons, and grapefruit the color of sunshine itself, but it also takes a lot of sunshine for citrus to grow. It makes sense that sunny Southern California was the birthplace of the commercial citrus industry in the state. Since citrus trees were first planted by mission padres in 1769, it was clear that the warm summers and mild winters of California created the perfect climate for these trees of golden fruit. The first commercial orchard was planted near Los Angeles in 1841. In the decades that followed, more groves were planted throughout Southern California and into the Central Valley. Some historians call this era the

Second Gold Rush, as growers and workers alike poured into the state to make a living in this new "golden" industry. Some even say it's part of what made California "The Golden State." No argument here!

Today, citrus trees are part of almost every backyard garden in Southern California. We grew grapefruit for years, our neighbor grows lemons, and my daughter just planted an orange tree. My parents had a prolific tree of a mystery citrus we jokingly called le'ranges. They were the color of lemons (almost) but tasted more like oranges. Whatever they were, they made the best juice!

A visit to the California Citrus State Historic Park in Riverside is *the* place to go to learn *everything* about citrus itself and the citrus industry. The knowledgeable staff offers tours, tastings, and occasional classes on growing, grafting, or cooking with citrus. A pleasant stroll along palm tree-lined paths takes you through groves of more than seventy kinds of citrus, from tiny kumquats to giant pomelos, and every type of orange or lemon along the way. The scent of orange blossoms is in the air and the surrounding views are lovely. A stop at the tiny, perfectly citrus themed, gift shop is a must, as is a stop at the fruit stand for fresh oranges and fresh squeezed juice. After our last visit to this park, we were so inspired that our family went home and created an entire citrus dinner, from Orange Broccoli Beef to Lemon-Glazed Cake—all recipes from a cookbook I bought in the gift shop, of course.

Using the freshest of citrus-inspired colors, this design features images of lemon slices and oranges combined with simple stripes and a patterned band of color. Try mixing up the colors a bit to feature *your* favorite citrus.

SIZE

One size fits an average adult size head (approx. 19 in. / 48 cm to 22 in. / 56 cm). Finished circumference: approx. 20¼ in. / 51.5 cm.

YARN

Worsted weight yarn (#4) in four colors. Shown in:

- **A:** Aly Bee Workshop Merino Worsted: Marmalade (25 g / 50 yd. / 46 m)

- **B:** Aly Bee Workshop Merino Worsted: Lemon Slices (25 g / 50 yd. / 46 m)

- **C:** Stunning String Studio Merino Worsted: Pasture (10 g / 22 yd. / 20 m)

- **D:** Malabrigo, Rios: Natural (25 g / 53 yd. / 49 m)

NEEDLES

- US size 5 / 3.75 mm, 16 in. / 40 cm circular knitting needles
- US size 7 / 4.5 mm, 16 in. / 40 cm circular knitting needles
- US size 7 / 4.5 mm set of double-pointed needles (DPNs) (or size needed to obtain gauge)

Continued on next page

NOTIONS

- 3 stitch markers (two of one color and one of another color)
- Tapestry needle for weaving in ends

GAUGE

With larger needles, approx. 9½ stitches = 2 in. / 5 cm in stranded stockinette stitch blocked.

Note: If you already know you are a tight knitter (or just want a larger hat), go up one or two needle sizes for both the ribbing and the body of the hat.

KNITTING INSTRUCTIONS

With smaller circular needles and color A, cast on 96 stitches. Place single color marker and join in the round, being careful not to twist stitches.

Work (k1, p1) ribbing pattern for 1½ to 2 in. / 4 to 5 cm.

Switch to larger needles and work chart from right to left beginning on Row 1, bottom right corner. Chart repeats three times around the hat. Use remaining two stitch markers of another color to mark chart repeats.

Note: In order to avoid long "floats" (strands of yarn on the inside of the hat) and to help maintain your tension, do not carry a color more than three or four stitches without twisting the colors around each other in the back of work.

Switch to DPNs when work becomes too small for circular needles.

FINISHING

After chart is complete, cut yarn, leaving a 10 in. / 25.5 cm tail. Using a tapestry needle, weave tail through remaining stitches and pull tightly to close circle. Pull tail to inside and weave in all ends.

Block as desired. See p. 12 for my favorite hat blocking technique.

KEY

■	A
□	B
■	C
□	D
□	K Knit
◪	K2tog Knit 2 together
■	No stitch **Note:** The "no stitch" squares are placeholders for stitches that are gained or lost throughout the design. *Do not skip a stitch.* Simply treat these squares as if they do not exist.

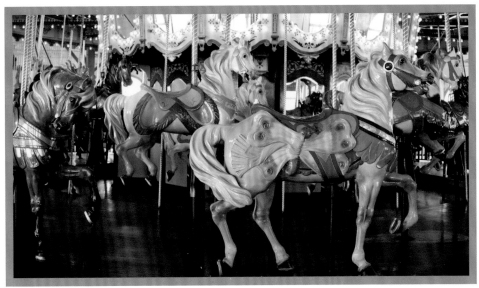

Theme Parks and Carousels

Did you know that July 25 is National Merry-Go-Round Day? These simple rides from a bygone era are definitely something to celebrate and are still found in almost every theme park in California and across the country! Even the inspiration for Disneyland (perhaps the most famous theme park of all) came to be as Walt Disney sat on a bench and watched his daughters ride the merry-go-round at Griffith Park in Los Angeles. Although the original inspiration for merry-go-rounds, also known as carousels, likely came from jousting matches in the twelfth century, the theme park rides we recognize today first appeared in the U.S. around 1800.

From that time through the early 1930s, thousands of carousels popped up across the county. Folks of all ages and from all walks of life experienced the simple joy of riding up and down and round and round. Over the years, carousels became increasingly elaborate, decorated with colorful hand-carved and painted animals, murals and mirrors, and, of course, the addition of the lively music we all love. Thankfully, many of these original rides have been preserved as historical landmarks.

In today's world of theme parks filled with thrill-seeking, upside-down roller coasters, there's still something magical about a simple ride on a colorful carousel. Perhaps it's the lifelong memories associated with them. They are often the first ride that parents take their young toddlers on, strapped into the saddle together or lovingly standing alongside holding tight as their giggling child goes up and down. Being old enough to ride alone is a rite of passage in itself. As a teenager, riding and laughing with friends or holding hands from horse to horse with a special someone makes the ride feel completely different. For adults, they're a welcome and calming break from the hurry of everyday life. Even now, as I watch or ride a carousel, it takes me back to childhood, remembering the excitement of being old enough to ride alone. Patiently waiting in line for my turn, I watched the colorful horses and animals go round and round before making my choice of the one I wanted to ride. What a thrill it was when my chosen one was available! Even better if the horse started or ended in the "up" position. The struggle of climbing on or off of something just a little too high made it all the more fun. Whether the carousel in your home state or in your memories is vintage or brand-new, the nostalgia of riding one is the same.

This colorful and fun design was inspired by the vintage carousels found from San Diego, Griffith Park, and Disneyland to the famous Santa Monica pier and Chase Palm Park in Santa Barbara. Simple stranded knitting features a colorful awning atop a carousel of galloping horses waiting for a touch of embroidery that makes each one a little different.

SIZE

One size fits an average adult size head (approx. 19 in. / 48 cm to 22 in. / 56 cm) Finished circumference: approx. 20¼ in. / 51.5 cm.

YARN

Worsted weight yarn (#4) in five colors. Shown in Aly Bee Workshop Merino Worsted in the following colors:

- **A:** Harvest (33 g / 66 yd. / 60 m)
- **B:** Picnic Weather (15 g / 30 yd. / 27 m)
- **C:** Orchard (5 g / 10 yd. / 9 m)
- **D:** Lichen (33 g / 66 yd. / 60 m)
- **E:** Sweet Cream (15 g / 30 yd. / 27 m)

Optional: A few yards each of any yarns in assorted colors for adding extra decorations to the horses. A few yards of any gold metallic thread or yarn to add a spiral design to the poles.

NEEDLES

- US size 5 / 3.75 mm, 16 in. / 40 cm circular knitting needles
- US size 7 / 4.5 mm, 16 in. / 40 cm circular knitting needles
- US size 7 / 4.5 mm set of double-pointed needles (DPNs) (or size needed to obtain gauge)

Continued on next page

- 3 stitch markers (two of one color and one of another color)
- Tapestry needle for weaving in ends and working duplicate stitches and embroidery

GAUGE

With larger needles, approx. 9½ stitches = 2 in. / 5 cm in stranded stockinette stitch blocked.

Note: If you already know you are a tight knitter (or just want a larger hat), go up one or two needle sizes for both the ribbing and the body of the hat.

KNITTING INSTRUCTIONS

With smaller circular needles and color A, cast on 96 stitches. Place single color marker and join in the round, being careful not to twist stitches.

Work (k2, p2) ribbing pattern for 1½ to 2 in. / 4 to 5 cm.

Switch to larger needles and work chart from right to left beginning on Row 1, bottom right corner. Chart repeats three times around the hat. Use remaining two stitch markers of another color to mark chart repeats.

Note: In order to avoid long "floats" (strands of yarn on the inside of the hat) and to help maintain your tension, do not carry a color more than three or four stitches without twisting the colors around each other in the back of work.

Switch to DPNs when work becomes too small for circular needles.

FINISHING

After chart is complete, cut yarn, leaving a 10 in. / 25.5 cm tail. Using a tapestry needle, weave tail through remaining stitches and pull tightly to close circle. Pull tail to inside and weave in all ends.

Block as desired. See p. 12 for my favorite hat blocking technique.

Duplicate stitches: After all other knitting is complete, add duplicate stitches to create poles where shown using color A or any other desired color.

Optional: Using any colors of scrap yarn, add decorations and personality to the horses with simple straight stitches and French knots (see p. 185). Beads or buttons could also add a fun touch. I used a gold metallic yarn to add a swirling effect to the poles. Use your imagination and have fun with it. See photos for inspiration.

KEY

- ☐ A
- ☐ B
- ☐ C
- ☐ D
- ☐ E
- ☐ K
  Knit
- D Duplicate Stitch
  To be done after all other knitting is complete
- ╱ K2tog
  Knit 2 together
- ■ No stitch
  Note: The "no stitch" squares are placeholders for stitches that are gained or lost throughout the design. *Do not skip a stitch.* Simply treat these squares as if they do not exist.

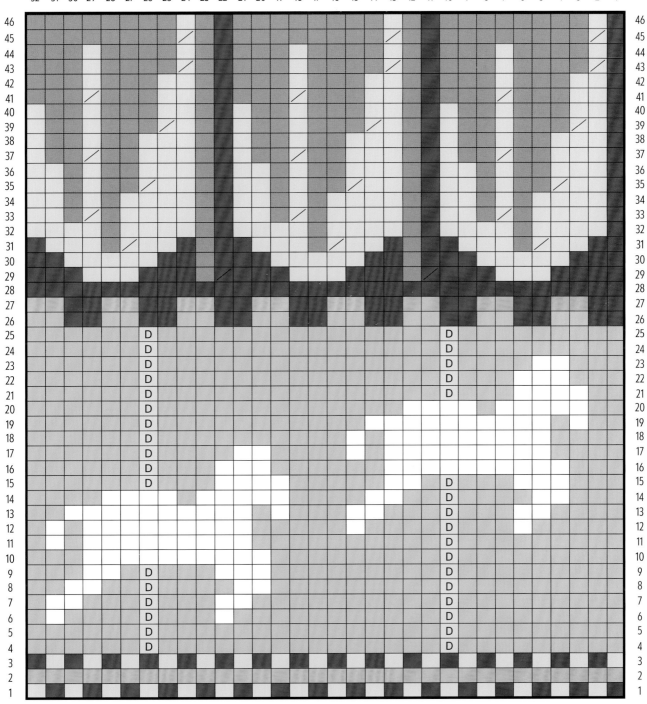

CENTRAL
CALIFORNIA

Gold Country

THERE'S GOLD IN CALIFORNIA! When James Marshall unexpectedly discovered gold at Sutter's Mill in January of 1848 in the Sierra Nevada foothills, nobody expected it would lead to one of the greatest mass migrations in U.S. history. News of the discovery was slow to spread at first. Many even doubted its authentencity. But, by 1849, as word of mouth, personal letters, and newspaper headlines spread the news like wildfire, the California gold rush was on! Thousands of ambitious prospectors (mostly men) flocked to California with the dream of striking it rich. Gold Fever was in full swing!

Dozens of boomtowns popped up throughout the area to support the growing number of "49ers" (as the prospectors were later called). Although many miners did indeed find a fortune in gold, many more found their fortunes in the business of supporting the miners. After all, everyone needed food, clothing, and supplies to keep the prospecting going. Even Levi Strauss, of the famous jean company, began his legacy by selling dry goods to miners, lumberjacks, and farmers. By the mid-1850s, the gold was basically gone, but the growth in the economy (and many of the boomtowns) were here to stay.

Traveling through Gold Country today is a mix of charming little towns (with shops, restaurants, and wineries) and a living history lesson—with lots of beautiful scenery mixed in. In fact, the small, historic town of Murphys is just minutes away from Calavaras Big Trees State Park, where you can hike among giant sequoias. Throughout the towns of the Gold Country region, historic buildings, mine tours, and even gold-panning lessons give visitors a firsthand glimpse into the life of the 49ers. When I was a child, my parents went through a gold-panning phase for a couple of years. Gold pans in hand, we stopped at rivers and streams, scooped up handfuls of gravel, and swished and swirled the water to our hearts content. I'm convinced that any gold in those pans would have been tossed out in the process! Not surprisingly, we never found gold. But we definitely struck it rich in family memories.

Using simple colorwork, this design takes you to the heart of Gold Country from the gravel of the river bottom to the blue sky above foothills and tall pine trees. Look at all the gold in that river! With or without the optional gold, the nature-inspired colors and classic shapes depict a scene reminiscent of many a mountain adventure.

SIZE

One size fits an average adult size head (approx. 19 in. / 48 cm to 22 in. / 56 cm) Finished circumference: approx. 20¼ in. / 51.5 cm.

YARN

Worsted weight yarn (#4) in five colors plus "Gold" as described below. Shown in:

☐ **A:** Western Sky Knits, Merino 17 Worsted: Peppered (50 g / 93 yd. / 85 m)

◼ **B:** Stunning String Studio Legacy Worsted: Big Sky (10 g / 22 yd. / 20 m)

☐ **C:** Aly Bee Workshop Merino Worsted: Prickly Pear (10 g / 20 yd. / 18 m)

◼ **D:** Stunning String Studio Legacy Worsted: Deep Forest (20 g/ 43 yd. / 39 m)

☐ **E:** Peekaboo Yarns Merino Worsted: Everglades Blue (20 g / 44 yd. / 40 m)

☐ **F:** Color B and Gold* held together

Gold: To add some realistic "gold" to the river bottom, you'll need to knit with a gold yarn *along with* color B, holding both strands together. I used Lana Grossa Brillino: Color 3, Gold (thread weight, #0). You can use *any* sparkly gold metallic thread/ yarn as long as it isn't any heavier than fingering weight (#1). The addition of the gold yarn on some of the stitches in the river might make your gauge just a tad larger for these few rows, but it is not significant enough to alter the size of the hat.

Continued on next page

NEEDLES

- US size 5 / 3.75 mm, 16 in. / 40 cm circular knitting needles
- US size 7 / 4.5 mm, 16 in. / 40 cm circular knitting needles
- US size 7 / 4.5 mm set of double-pointed needles (DPNs) (or size needed to obtain gauge)

NOTIONS

- 3 stitch markers (two of one color and one of another color)
- Tapestry needle for weaving in ends
- Optional: Faux-fur pom-pom

GAUGE

With larger needles, approx. 9½ stitches = 2 in. / 5 cm in stranded stockinette stitch blocked.

Note: If you already know you are a tight knitter (or just want a larger hat), go up one or two needle sizes for both the ribbing and the body of the hat.

KNITTING INSTRUCTIONS

With smaller circular needles and color A, cast on 96 stitches. Place single color marker and join in the round, being careful not to twist stitches.

Work (k1, p1) ribbing pattern for 3½ to 4 in. / 9 to 10 cm for a double layer (fold-over) or 1½ to 2 in. / 4 to 5 cm for a single layer.

Increase Round: *K31, k in front and back of next stitch (kfb); repeat from * two more times— 99 stitches total.

Switch to larger needles and work chart from right to left beginning on Row 1, bottom right corner. Chart repeats three times around the hat. Use remaining two stitch markers of another color to mark chart repeats.

Note: In order to avoid long "floats" (strands of yarn on the inside of the hat) and to help maintain your tension, do not carry a color more than three or four stitches without twisting the colors around each other in the back of work.

Switch to DPNs when work becomes too small for circular needles.

FINISHING

After chart is complete, cut yarn, leaving a 10 in. / 25.5 cm tail. Using a tapestry needle, weave tail through remaining stitches and pull tightly to close circle. Pull tail to inside and weave in all ends.

Block as desired. See p. 12 for my favorite hat blocking technique.

Optional: Add a purchased faux-fur pom-pom to top of hat.

KEY

⬜	A
⬜	B
⬜	C
⬛	D
⬜	E
⬜	F
⬜	K Knit
◩	K2tog Knit 2 together
⬛	No stitch **Note:** The "no stitch" squares are placeholders for stitches that are gained or lost throughout the design. *Do not skip a stitch.* Simply treat these squares as if they do not exist.
⬜	**Important:** The yellow squares represent color B (the river) and a gold yarn held together. Do NOT knit these squares with the gold yarn alone. Simply carry the gold along the back as you knit and then pick it up and knit together with B where shown. Feel free to add less or more gold as desired, keeping in mind that gold is heavier than water and tends to sink to the bottom of the river.

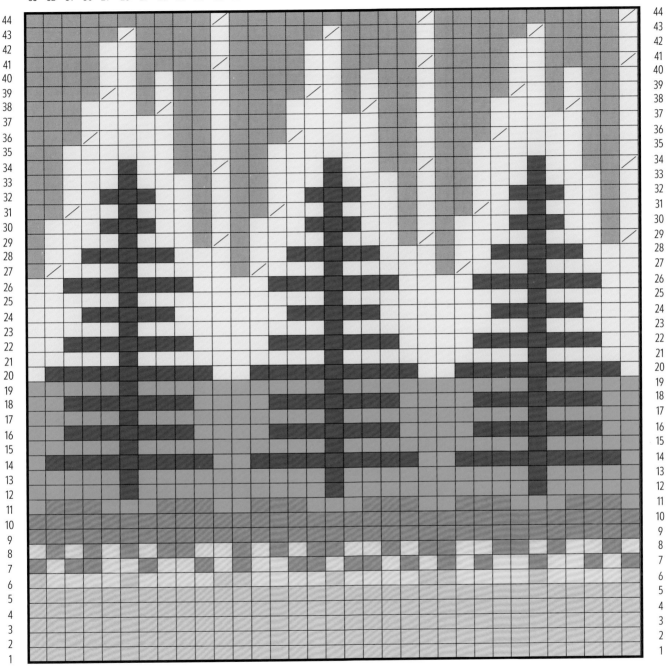

The Central Valley

It's been called the Big Valley, the Breadbasket of California, the Great Valley, and even the Golden Empire. To many, it's simply The Valley—miles and miles and rows and rows of agriculture as far as the eye can see! To novelist John Steinbeck, it was the setting for several of his classic stories. But, to anyone road-tripping along Interstate 5 (simply "the 5" to most Californians) through the heart of the state, the Central Valley becomes a fun guessing game of what's growing on either side of the road. Pink or white blossoms on the trees? Maybe it's nectarines, peaches, or nuts. Is that lettuce? Asparagus? Sometimes the scent of onions or garlic is so strong, there's no mystery!

Almost three hundred different crops grow in the farmlands of this flat fertile valley, producing a large percentage of the country's vegetables, fruits, nuts, and cotton. The area runs 450 miles / 725 km from Bakersfield in the south to Redding in the north, with highways 5 and 99 running right down the middle. The valley is just 40 to 50 miles / 65 to 80 km wide and flanked by the Sierra Nevada range on the east and the Coastal Range on the west. On a clear day, you can see the mountains on either side of the valley. A drive through the area is relaxing, perfect for road-trip knitting, and even a bit mesmerizing as you pass by acres of neatly planted rows. And, if your timing is right, a side trip could include strawberry pie, garlic ice cream, bacon-wrapped asparagus, or peach lemonade, as many of the local communities embrace their agricultural roots with yearly food festivals. Yum!

My first trip in an airplane (at age fourteen) took me directly over the Central Valley. I was immediately struck by the vastness of the area and how it took on an entirely different look when viewed from above. This new perspective revealed patterns that could only be seen from the air. The huge, carefully mapped-out parcels of farmland looked like the squares of a giant quilt spread out over the land. I was awestruck! Every flight since that first has left the same impression. It never gets old!

This easy-to-knit design was inspired by that memorable view from above—stripes of plowed rows, recently harvested or newly planted fields, and the fun patterns they create. Just three colors of greens and golds evoke the look of acres of crops. But the fun checkerboard pattern itself would look amazing in any three colors.

SIZE
One size fits an average adult size head (approx. 19 in. / 48 cm to 22 in. / 56 cm). Finished circumference: approx. 20¼ in. / 51.5 cm.

YARN
Worsted weight yarn (#4) in three colors. Shown in:

☐ **A:** Aly Bee Workshop Merino Worsted: Fresh Cut (50 g / 100 yd. / 91 m)

☐ **B:** Aly Bee Workshop Merino Worsted: Harvest (25 g / 50 yd. / 46 m)

☐ **C:** Malabrigo, Rios: Yerba (25 g / 53 yd. / 49 m)

NEEDLES
- US size 5 / 3.75 mm, 16 in. / 40 cm circular knitting needles
- US size 7 / 4.5 mm, 16 in. / 40 cm circular knitting needles
- US size 7 / 4.5 mm set of double-pointed needles (DPNs) (or size needed to obtain gauge)

Continued on next page

KNITTING INSTRUCTIONS

With smaller circular needles and color A, cast on 96 stitches. Place single color marker and join in the round, being careful not to twist stitches.

Work (k1, p1) ribbing pattern for 1½ to 2 in. / 4 to 5 cm.

Switch to larger needles and work chart from right to left beginning on Row 1, bottom right corner. Chart repeats three times around the hat. Use remaining two stitch markers of another color to mark chart repeats.

Note: In order to avoid long "floats" (strands of yarn on the inside of the hat) and to help maintain your tension, do not carry a color more than three or four stitches without twisting the colors around each other in the back of work.

Switch to DPNs when work becomes too small for circular needles.

FINISHING

After chart is complete, cut yarn, leaving a 10 in. / 25.5 cm tail. Using a tapestry needle, weave tail through remaining stitches and pull tightly to close circle. Pull tail to inside and weave in all ends.

Block as desired. See p. 12 for my favorite hat blocking technique.

KEY

⬜	A
⬜	B
⬜	C
⬜	K Knit
◪	K2tog Knit 2 together
◩	SSK Slip, Slip, Knit: Slip 2 stitches knitwise, place stitches back on left needle, knit 2 tog through back loop
⬛	No stitch

Note: The "no stitch" squares are placeholders for stitches that are gained or lost throughout the design. *Do not skip a stitch.* Simply treat these squares as if they do not exist.

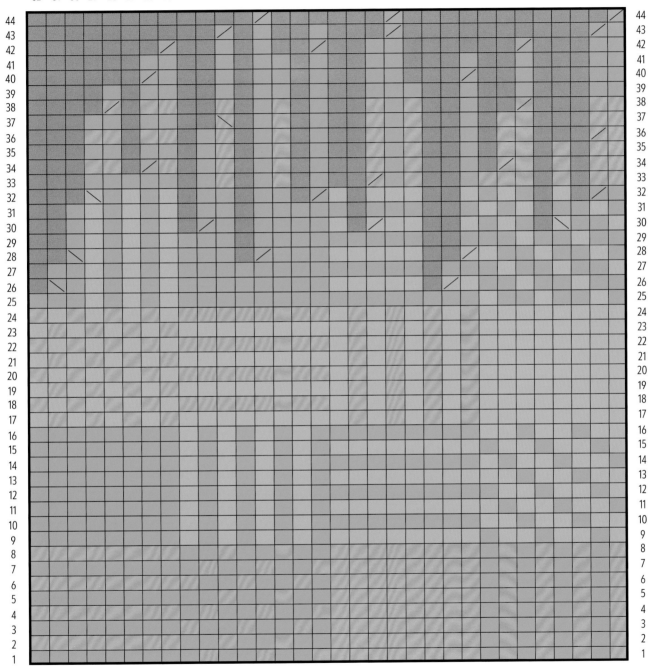

The Eastern Sierras

Imagine it's the 1930s and you (the location scout for a major motion picture company) have been assigned the task of finding the perfect filming location for the next big western. The criteria? Rugged yet beautiful terrain, clear skies, great weather, and lots of open space. To stay within budget, the producers need an area with valleys, trees, lakes, and rivers, but it also needs to pass for a desert. A nearby town for the cast and crew with close access to a railroad would be perfect. Oh . . . and all of this with a majestic backdrop of snowcapped mountains. Does such a place exist? It certainly does. Welcome to the Eastern Sierras!

Since the early 1930s, hundreds of movies have been filmed in the Eastern Sierras, from *Gunga Din* and *The Lone Ranger* to *Gladiator*, *Tremors*, and *Iron Man*. Why is the east so different from the west? When viewing the Sierra Nevada range from the west, the mountains seem far, far away. Even as you drive up the curvy roads, it's a very gradual process. You can't really sense you're getting higher until the pine trees start to appear and your ears begin to plug from the altitude. But the view from the *east* is entirely different. The huge mountain range seems to jut directly from the valley below, creating the perfect natural backdrop for filmmaking while the diversity of terrain suits a multitude of settings. Even as my geologist daughter explains the science behind the shapes of the mountains, it all seems miraculous to me! In fact, the drive through the valley along the 395 from Olancha in the south to Bridgeport in the north has become one of my family's favorite road trips. Nestled between Sequoia, Kings Canyon, and Yosemite National Parks on the west and Death Valley on the east, the area is filled with hidden gems you can't see from the highway. A stop at the Tufa formations at Mono Lake feels like a trip to the moon while the Ancient Bristlecone Pine Forest takes you thousands of years back in time. You can explore a volcanic cone, soak in hot springs, dine on great barbecue, or picnic near a tiny lake. In the autumn, beautiful fall foliage appears across the valley. Visits to Laws Railroad Museum and the Museum of Western Film History are must-dos. One of my favorite areas (*full* of moviemaking history) is Alabama Hills, the boulder-filled, desert-like area near Lone Pine off of Whitney Portal Road (the gateway to Mount Whitney). Miles of unpaved roads surrounded by boulders of all sizes offer up different views around every corner. The mostly rounded rock formations (caused by millions of years of spheroidal weathering) create fun shapes that inspire the imagination and invite exploration.

In the beautiful colors of the Eastern Sierras, this design hints at the texture of Alabama Hills against a backdrop of mountains and sky. The small arch represents Mobius Arch, the natural rock formation that (in real life) perfectly frames Mount Whitney in the distance.

SIZE

One size fits an average adult size head (approx. 19 in. / 48 cm to 22 in. / 56 cm). Finished circumference: approx. 20¼ in. / 51.5 cm.

YARN

Worsted weight yarn (#4) in five colors. Shown in:

- **A:** Malabrigo Rios: Camel (50 g / 105 yd. / 96 m)
- **B:** Aly Bee Workshop Merino Worsted: Prickly Pear (10 g / 20 yd. / 18 m))
- **C:** Malabrigo Rios: Winter Lake (15 g / 32 yd. / 29 m)
- **D:** Malabrigo Rios: Natural (15 g / 32 yd. / 29 m)
- **E:** Stunning String Studio Legacy Worsted: Cloudy Sky (10 g / 22 yd. / 20 m)

NEEDLES

- US size 5 / 3.75 mm, 16 in. / 40 cm circular knitting needles
- US size 7 / 4.5 mm, 16 in. / 40 cm circular knitting needles
- S US size 7 / 4.5 mm set of double-pointed needles (DPNs) (or size needed to obtain gauge)

Continued on next page

NOTIONS

- 3 stitch markers (two of one color and one of another color)
- Cable needle
- Tapestry needle for weaving in ends

GAUGE

With larger needles, approx. 9½ stitches = 2 in. / 5 cm in stranded stockinette stitch blocked.

Note: If you already know you are a tight knitter (or just want a larger hat), go up one or two needle sizes for both the ribbing and the body of the hat.

KNITTING INSTRUCTIONS

With smaller circular needles and color A, cast on 96 stitches. Place single color marker and join in the round, being careful not to twist stitches.

Work (k1, p1) ribbing pattern for 1½ to 2 in. / 4 to 5 cm.

Switch to larger needles and work chart from right to left beginning on Row 1, bottom right corner. Chart repeats three times around the hat. Use remaining two stitch markers of another color to mark chart repeats.

Note: In order to avoid long "floats" (strands of yarn on the inside of the hat) and to help maintain your tension, do not carry a color more than three or four stitches without twisting the colors around each other in the back of work.

Switch to DPNs when work becomes too small for circular needles.

FINISHING

After chart is complete, cut yarn, leaving a 10 in. / 25.5 cm tail. Using a tapestry needle, weave tail through remaining stitches and pull tightly to close circle. Pull tail to inside and weave in all ends.

Block as desired. See p. 12 for my favorite hat blocking technique.

KEY

- ■ A
- ▨ B
- ▨ C
- □ D
- ▨ E
- □ K
  Knit
- ⊡ P
  Purl
- ⬤ Mb
  Make Bobble: (P1, k1, p1, k1) into next stitch, then lift 2nd, 3rd, and 4th stitches over first stitch and off needle, one at a time
- ☑ S1
  Slip 1 purl-wise with yarn in back
- ⊿ K2tog
  Knit 2 together
- 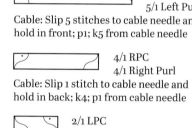 5/1 LPC
  5/1 Left Purl
  Cable: Slip 5 stitches to cable needle and hold in front; p1; k5 from cable needle
- 4/1 RPC
  4/1 Right Purl
  Cable: Slip 1 stitch to cable needle and hold in back; k4; p1 from cable needle
- 2/1 LPC
  2/1 Left Purl Cable: Slip 2 stitches to cable needle and hold in front; p1; k2 from cable needle
- PFB
  Purl Front and Back: Purl into the front of the stitch, leaving the stitch on the needle, and then purl into the back of the same stitch
- ◩ s2tog-k2tog-p2sso
  Slip 2 stitches together knitwise, knit 2 together, then pass 2 slipped stitches over and off of needle
- ■ No stitch
  Note: The "no stitch" squares are placeholders for stitches that are gained or lost throughout the design. *Do not skip a stitch.* Simply treat these squares as if they do not exist

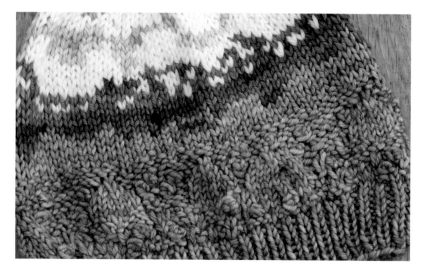

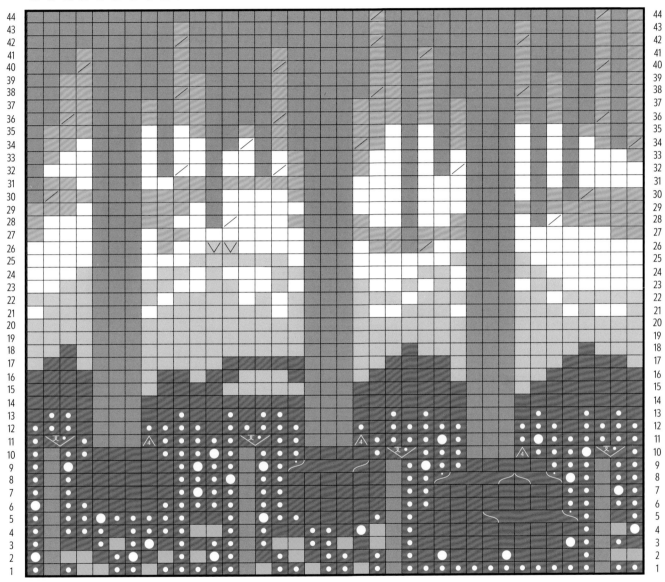

Mammoth Mountain

High in the Eastern Sierras of California, in the heart of a beautiful and picturesque region of year-round adventures, lies Mammoth Mountain—an 11,000 foot / 3,350 m volcano at the edge of the Long Valley Caldera. The entire area, just ten minutes or so off the main highway, is a visual gem! Nearly 400 inches / 1,000 cm of snow and up to three hundred days of sunshine a year combine to create an ideal setting for adventures of every type in every season. In the spring, snowmelt feeds rivers, waterfalls, and lakes as wildflowers sprout in green meadows. In summer, temperatures warm and campgrounds open while hikers and mountain bikers are out in full force. It's a great to time to hop on the shuttle or hike

to Devils Postpile National Monument, one of the world's finest examples of columnar basalt columns. The autumn brings spectacular fall colors and cooler days.

Mammoth is one of our favorite stops on our annual fall foliage drive through the Eastern Sierras. The yellows and oranges against snowcapped peaks are spectacular! As winter sets in, a snow-covered playground appears. Mammoth contains the highest ski resort in California, which is considered by many to be one of the best in the world. Even non-skiers like me can easily enjoy what winter has to offer. Scenic gondola rides take visitors to the top of the mountain in winter (and in summer) for spectacular views. We took our first winter trip to Mammoth this year to take photos of this hat. As a Southern Californian, I can honestly say, I've never seen so much snow! When we pulled off the rode and walked into the forest a bit to take photos, I was surprised to see large, well-maintained cross-country skiing trails. I was impressed by how well the trails just blended in with the scenery. It was perfect! The huge pine trees were covered with snow and looked just like the flocked trees you see in Christmas tree lots. Occasional gusts of wind blew snow off the trees and landed on us in magical swirls. All this snow probably seems commonplace to some people (well, a *lot* of people), but to someone who doesn't see it a lot or live in it, I could truly appreciate it for the winter wonderland it was.

In the classic colors of Mammoth (blue and white), this design features snow-covered trees in a snowy landscape. A fold-over ribbing, a patterned band reminiscient of snowfall, and an optional faux-fur pom-pom complete the look of this classic-style winter hat.

SIZE

One size fits an average adult size head (approx. 19 in. / 48 cm to 22 in. / 56 cm). Finished circumference: approx. 20¼ in. / 51.5 cm.

YARN

Worsted weight yarn (#4) in two colors. Shown in:

- ☐ **A:** Malabrigo Rios: Natural (50 g / 105 yd. / 96 m)
- ■ **B:** Aly Bee Workshop Merino Worsted: Picnic Weather (50 g / 100 yd. / 91 m)

NEEDLES

- US size 5 / 3.75 mm, 16 in. / 40 cm circular knitting needles
- US size 7 / 4.5 mm, 16 in. / 40 cm circular knitting needles
- US size 7 / 4.5 mm set of double-pointed needles (DPNs) (or size needed to obtain gauge)

NOTIONS

- 3 stitch markers (two of one color and one of another color)
- Tapestry needle for weaving in ends
- Optional: Faux-fur pom-pom

Continued on next page

KNITTING INSTRUCTIONS

With smaller circular needles and color A, cast on 96 stitches. Place single color marker and join in the round, being careful not to twist stitches.

Work (k1, p1) ribbing pattern for a 3½ in. to 4 in. / 9 to 10 cm for a double layer (fold-over) ribbing or 1½ to 2 in. / 4 to 5 cm for a single layer ribbing.

Increase Round: *K31, k in front and back of next stitch (kfb); repeat from * two more times—99 stitches total.

Switch to larger needles and work chart from right to left beginning on Row 1, bottom right corner. Chart repeats three times around the hat. Use remaining two stitch markers of another color to mark chart repeats.

Note: In order to avoid long "floats" (strands of yarn on the inside of the hat) and to help maintain your tension, do not carry a color more than three or four stitches without twisting the colors around each other in the back of work.

Switch to DPNs when work becomes too small for circular needles.

FINISHING

After chart is complete, cut yarn, leaving a 10 in. / 25.5 cm tail. Using a tapestry needle, weave tail through remaining stitches and pull tightly to close circle. Pull tail to inside and weave in all ends.

Block as desired. See p. 12 for my favorite hat blocking technique.

Optional: Add a purchased faux-fur pom-pom to top of hat.

KEY

☐	A
▨	B
☐	K Knit
◩	SSK Slip, Slip, Knit: Slip 2 stitches knitwise, place stitches back on left needle, knit 2 tog through back loop
◩	K2tog Knit 2 together
◼	No stitch **Note:** The "no stitch" squares are placeholders for stitches that are gained or lost throughout the design. *Do not skip a stitch.* Simply treat these squares as if they do not exist.

Dark Sky Giants

You know how some things seem smaller when viewed as an adult than you remember them as a child? It's that feeling of "I remember this house being much bigger when I was a kid." Well, giant sequoias aren't one of those things! No matter how young you were when you saw these huge trees for the first time, each time you see them, even decades later, they will be just as giant and incredible as you remember. They are virtually unchanged and the only hint at the passage of time is you, your kids, friends, and family. Photos of my daughters from several trips to Sequoia National Park over the years are among some of my favorites to look back on. Watching them grow up and change against a natural backdrop that doesn't reminds me of how short our lives are compared

to those trees. The giant sequoias found in Sequoia, Kings Canyon, and Yosemite National Parks as well as Calavaras Big Trees State Park are the largest trees in the world! The term *large* seems entirely inadequate when you're standing next to one with a diameter wider than a city street and a height so tall, you can't see the top!

While sequoias are the *largest* trees by volume (huge trunks!) the coastal redwoods of California are the *tallest*. Both species are giants by any description and completely awe-inspiring. It's no surprise that visitors come from around the world to experience these great wonders of nature. They are amazing in any season! The green meadows and wildflowers of spring and summer, the warmth of changing leaves on smaller trees in the fall, and the snow-covered landscape in winter offer different backdrops for viewing these spectacular trees. But one of the most memorable views is that of giant sequoias silhouetted against a star-studded night sky. Whether you're taking in the scene from the porch of a cabin or from a sleeping bag under the stars, the unforgettable view is worth every moment of staying up just a little later than planned.

Using only two colors and simple stranded colorwork, this beanie features the black silhouettes of sequoias and other trees against the night sky with optional beaded stars. The "stars" are simple silver seed beads with a few larger sparkly ones to represent the stars, galaxies, and planets that stand out from the others. The quantity and placement of beads is completely up to you.

SIZE

One size fits an average adult size head (approx. 19 in. / 48 cm to 22 in. / 56 cm). Finished circumference: approx. 20¼ in. / 51.5 cm.

YARN

Worsted weight yarn (#4) in two colors. Shown in:

- ■ **A:** Stunning String Studio Legacy Worsted: Little Black Dress (50 g / 108 yd. / 99 m)
- ■ **B:** Malabrigo Rios: Azules (50 g / 105 yd. / 96 m)

NEEDLES

- US size 5 / 3.75 mm, 16 in. / 40 cm circular knitting needles
- US size 7 / 4.5 mm, 16 in. / 40 cm circular knitting needles
- US size 7 / 4.5 mm set of double-pointed needles (DPNs) (or size needed to obtain gauge)

NOTIONS

- 3 stitch markers (two of one color and one of another color)
- Silver or sparkly beads for the "stars" (optional)
- Small crochet hook or embroidery needle appropriate to the size of bead chosen for applying beads (optional)
- Embroidery floss or heavy-duty sewing thread in complementary color(s) for sewing on beads (optional)
- Tapestry needle for weaving in ends

Continued on next page

With larger needles, approx. 9½ stitches = 2 in. / 5 cm in stranded stockinette stitch blocked.

Note: If you already know you are a tight knitter (or just want a larger hat), go up one or two needle sizes for both the ribbing and the body of the hat.

KNITTING INSTRUCTIONS

With smaller circular needles and color A, cast on 96 stitches. Place single color marker and join in the round, being careful not to twist stitches.

Work the following ribbing pattern for 1½ to 2 in. / 4 to 5 cm.
Ribbing Pattern: *P1, k1, p2, k2, p2, k1, p2, k2, p1, k2, p1, k3, p3, k3, p2, k2, p2; repeat from * 2 more times.

Read carefully through the following instructions before beginning if planning to add beads to your project during knitting.

Switch to larger needles and work chart from right to left beginning on Row 1, bottom right corner. Chart repeats three times around the hat. Use remaining two stitch markers of another color to mark chart repeats.

To add optional bead "stars": If desired, add beads to your hat to create stars in the sky. Beads can be added randomly while knitting using the crochet hook or stringing method (see p. 184), or may be sewn onto the hat after all knitting and blocking is complete (to sew beads on after hat is complete, see Optional Stars at right). Add as many or as few as you'd like. You can even create your favorite constellation! I used #6 seed beads and a few larger crystal beads. Bead placement is completely up to you and not indicated on the chart.

Note: In order to avoid long "floats" (strands of yarn on the inside of the hat) and to help maintain your tension, do not carry a color more than three or four stitches without twisting the colors around each other in the back of work.

Switch to DPNs when work becomes too small for circular needles.

FINISHING

After chart is complete, cut yarn, leaving a 10 in. / 25.5 cm tail. Using a tapestry needle, weave tail through remaining stitches and pull tightly to close circle. Pull tail to inside and weave in all ends,

Block as desired. See p. 12 for my favorite hat blocking technique.

Optional Stars: After all blocking is complete, sew bead "stars" to your sky using an embroidery needle that fits through the bead. If the yarn seems too thick for sewing on beads, try separating the strands and only use one or two plies to attach the beads. Embroidery floss or heavy-duty thread also works well.

KEY

■	A
▨	B
☐	K Knit
☑ (V)	S1 Slip 1 purl-wise with yarn in back.
▨ (/)	K2tog Knit 2 together
■	No stitch **Note:** The "no stitch" squares are placeholders for stitches that are gained or lost throughout the design. *Do not skip a stitch.* Simply treat these squares as if they do not exist

California Poppies

A drive almost anywhere in California in the springtime is bound to include multiple sightings of California poppies, the brilliant orange state flower. In cities and towns, they grow along freeways, in vacant lots, on hillsides, in planters, and even in cracks in the sidewalks. Out in nature, state parks, valleys, canyons, mountainsides, and meadows become a canvas of orange, in pockets of growth and sometimes in vast swaths of color. One of the most impressive and memorable ways to experience these sunny flowers is a stroll through Antelope Valley California Poppy Reserve in the Western Mojave Desert. The reserve boasts 8 miles / 13 km of trails through the most consistent poppy-growing region in the state. Although the plants are protected from livestock grazing, everything else is left up to nature. Once poppies start growing, they'll pop up again every year if left to their own devices. In the spring, that first little glimpse of silvery green foliage lets you know the color explosion is just around the corner. For years, orange poppies sprung up in our backyard between rocks and in planters. A few even sprung up in the lawn! After spotting a plant with all white blooms one year and another with all yellow, my husband purchased seeds for all the colors of poppies he could find. Some of them took and some didn't, but from then on, among all the orange, there was always at least one with white blooms and one with yellow.

Poppies are not only great to look at, but they serve important purposes as well. They attract bees and butterfies, which helps with pollination of crops and flowers; you'll also often find them planted in vineyards and gardens to help keep nutrients in the soil.

The California poppy was enthusiastically selected as the state flower in 1890. Although poppies come in many colors, it's the common orange/yellow variety (in the color of sunshine itself) that so appropriately represents the state and is most seen growing in the wild. You'll find images of these orange beauties on welcome signs, T-shirts, mugs, beautiful artwork—and now on your own knitted hat.

This design uses stranded colorwork and a touch of duplicate stitching to create a band of brilliant orange poppies and poppy buds against a neutral backdrop and the perfect shade of desaturated green.

SIZE

One size fits an average adult size head (approx. 19 in. / 48 cm to 22 in. / 56 cm). Finished circumference: approx. 20¼ in. / 51.5 cm.

YARN

Worsted weight yarn (#4) in four colors. Shown in:

☐ **A:** Aly Bee Workshop Merino Worsted: Prickly Pear (33 g / 66 yd. / 60 m)

☐ **B:** Aly Bee Workshop Merino Worsted: Kettle Corn (25 g / 50 yd. / 46 m)

☐ **C:** Aly Bee Workshop Merino Worsted: Marmalade (20 g / 40 yd. / 37 m)

☐ **D:** Peekaboo Yarns Merino Worsted: Orange Blaze (10 g / 22 yd. / 20 m)

Optional: About 3 g / 6 yd. / 5 m each of any pink or yellow worsted weight (#4) yarn for embroidered blooms on the cactus

NEEDLES

- US size 5 / 3.75 mm, 16 in. / 40 cm circular knitting needles
- US size 7 / 4.5 mm, 16 in. / 40 cm circular knitting needles
- US size 7 / 4.5 mm set of double-pointed needles (DPNs) (or size needed to obtain gauge)

Continued on next page

NOTIONS

- 3 stitch markers (two of one color and one of another color)
- Tapestry needle for weaving in ends and working duplicate stitches

GAUGE

With larger needles, approx. 9½ stitches = 2 in. / 5 cm in stranded stockinette stitch blocked.

Note: If you already know you are a tight knitter (or just want a larger hat), go up one or two needle sizes for both the ribbing and the body of the hat.

KNITTING INSTRUCTIONS

With smaller circular needles and color A, cast on 96 stitches. Place single color marker and join in the round, being careful not to twist stitches.

Work (k1, p1) ribbing pattern for 1½ to 2 in. / 4 to 5 cm.

Switch to larger needles and work chart from right to left beginning on Row 1, bottom right corner. Chart repeats three times around the hat. Use remaining two stitch markers of another color to mark chart repeats.

Note: In order to avoid long "floats" (strands of yarn on the inside of the hat) and to help maintain your tension, do not carry a color more than three or four stitches without twisting the colors around each other in the back of work.

Switch to DPNs when work becomes too small for circular needles.

FINISHING

After chart is complete, cut yarn, leaving a 10 in. / 25.5 cm tail. Using a tapestry needle, weave tail through remaining stitches and pull tightly to close circle. Pull tail to inside and weave in all ends.

Block as desired. See p. 12 for my favorite hat blocking technique.

After all blocking is complete, work duplicate stitches where shown.

KEY

⬜	A
⬜	B
⬛	C
▨	D
⬜	K Knit
D	Duplicate Stitch To be done after all other knitting is complete
╱	K2tog Knit 2 together
⬛	No stitch **Note:** The "no stitch" squares are placeholders for stitches that are gained or lost throughout the design. *Do not skip a stitch.* Simply treat these squares as if they do not exist.

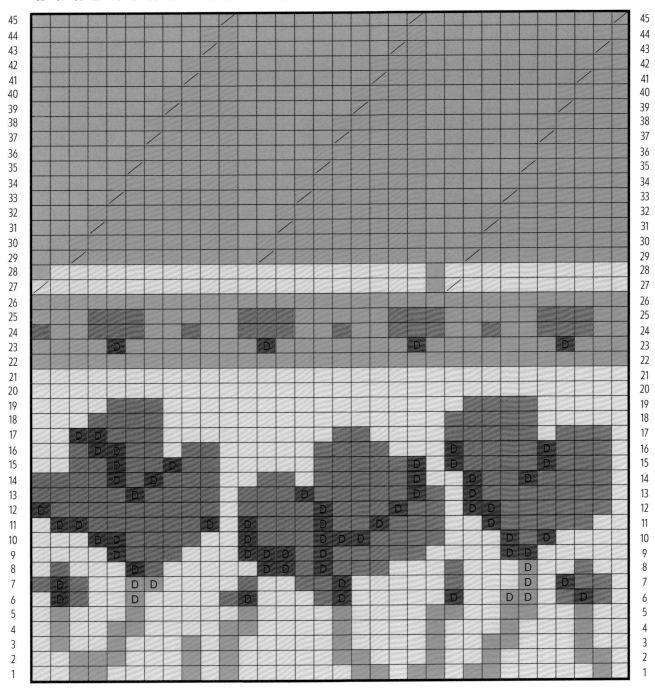

D	Knit this stitch in color B,	duplicate stitch in color A
D	Knit this stitch in color C,	duplicate stitch in color D

Death Valley

The largest of the nine California national parks, Death Valley also has the distinction of being the hottest, driest, and lowest of *all* sixty-three U.S national parks. It's these very conditions, along with billions of years of geologic forces and erosion, that have created the fascinating Death Valley landscape we know today. Someone who has never been there might ask, "Why would anyone go to such a place?" The list of reasons is as vast as the park itself!

In just one (preferably winter) day in Death Valley, you can explore a slot canyon, see a natural bridge, stroll along a boardwalk trail, drive the spectacular Artists Palette Road, (carefully) scramble over the jagged formations of Devils Golf Course, learn about the mining and borax

THE CENTRAL COAST

Pacific Coast Highway

Consistently ranked as one of the most beautiful drives in the country, Pacific Coast Highway (PCH) is both an engineering masterpiece and a scenic wonder. A journey along its entire 656-mile / 1,056 km length (almost the distance from Savannah, Georgia, to Lancaster, Pennsylvania) is a bucket-list item for many road-trip enthusiasts, including myself. What an adventure that would be! I've driven many sections several times, but never the entire route at once. The road trip is *so* iconic that dozens of books, blogs, and travel guides exist for the sole purpose of recommending things to do and see along the way. And, oh boy, is there a lot!

No matter which direction you choose to travel, the change in scenery is gradual and the terrain as diverse as the state of California itself. The route turns inland for a few stretches along the way, but overall, it is truly a coastal drive. The southern end takes you through famous beach towns such as Malibu and Santa Monica, and cities such as Long Beach and Los Angeles. Classic SoCal palm trees are everywhere! The denser traffic gradually gives way to more unobstructed views and relaxed driving. The palm trees fade away while grassy hillsides and rocky shores take over along the central coast through Pismo Beach, Moro Bay, and past San Simeon's famous Hearst Castle. The section a little further north through Big Sur is perhaps the most iconic and most photographed. The sea cliffs are higher, the winding road seems to cling to the edge as it crosses several famous bridges, and the views are nothing short of breathtaking. Strategically placed scenic overlooks are perfect for resting and snapping photos. The route continues through more seaside towns such as Monterey and Santa Cruz, then across Golden Gate Bridge in San Francisco, and up the northern coast through a dozen or so state parks, forests, and seashores—every one of them worthy of a stop. The California adventure ends near the northern border, but you can keep going through Oregon and Washington. Whether you take one week or four to travel the entire route, you'll never run out of amazing things to do or see. But, being on the West Coast, one sight is guaranteed no matter which section you travel— beautiful sunsets.

Inspired by my favorite section of PCH near Big Sur, this design captures the crashing surf against a rocky sea cliff with the road winding its way along the edge. Tiny straight stitches create the very important line down the center of the road, while a little blue car button (that looks a bit like my own car) makes its way up the coast.

SIZE

One size fits an average adult size head (approx. 19 in. / 48 cm to 22 in. / 56 cm). Finished circumference: approx. 20¼ in. / 51.5 cm.

YARN

Worsted weight yarn (#4) in seven colors (plus optional yellow). Shown in:

- ☐ **A:** Malabrigo, Rios: Denim (20 g / 42 yd. / 38 m)
- ☐ **B:** Malabrigo, Rios: Natural (10 g / 21 yd. / 19 m)
- ☐ **C:** Peekaboo Yarns Merino Worsted: Anacapa Island (10 g / 22 yd. / 20 m)
- ◼ **D:** Aly Bee Workshop Merino Worsted: Smoked (20 g / 40 yd. / 37 m)
- ☐ **E:** Malabrigo, Rios: Ivy (20 g / 42 yd. / 38 m)
- ☐ **F:** Peekaboo Yarns Merino Worsted: Silverstone (10 g / 22 yd. / 20 m)
- ◻ **G:** Polka Dot Sheep Whitefish Worsted: Moose Meadow (10 g / 22 yd. / 20 m)

Optional: A few yards of any yellow/yellow-gold worsted weight yarn (separated into single plies) to embroider line in street

NEEDLES

- US size 5 / 3.75 mm, 16 in. / 40 cm circular knitting needles
- US size 7 / 4.5 mm, 16 in. / 40 cm circular knitting needles
- US size 7 / 4.5 mm set of double-pointed needles (DPNs) (or size needed to obtain gauge)

Continued on next page

NOTIONS

- 3 stitch markers (two of one color and one of another color)
- Optional: Car-shaped button (or buttons) approx. ⅝ in / 1.5 cm
- Tapestry needle for weaving in ends and working duplicate stitches and embroidery

GAUGE

With larger needles, approx. 9½ stitches = 2 in. / 5 cm in stranded stockinette stitch blocked.

Note: If you already know you are a tight knitter (or just want a larger hat), go up one or two needle sizes for both the ribbing and the body of the hat.

KNITTING INSTRUCTIONS

With smaller circular needles and color A, cast on 96 stitches. Place single color marker and join in the round, being careful not to twist stitches.

Work {k1tbl (knit through back loop), p1} ribbing pattern for 1½ to 2 in. / 4 to 5 cm.

Switch to larger needles and work chart from right to left beginning on Row 1, bottom right corner. Chart repeats three times around the hat. Use remaining two stitch markers of another color to mark chart repeats.

Note: In order to avoid long "floats" (strands of yarn on the inside of the hat) and to help maintain your tension, do not carry a color more than three or four stitches without twisting the colors around each other in the back of work.

Switch to DPNs when work becomes too small for circular needles.

FINISHING

After chart is complete, cut yarn, leaving a 10 in. / 25.5 cm tail. Using a tapestry needle, weave tail through remaining stitches and pull tightly to close circle. Pull tail to inside and weave in all ends.

Block as desired. See p. 12 for my favorite hat blocking technique.

Work duplicate stitches where shown to create rocks along the shore.

Optional: With tapestry needle and a single ply of yellow yarn, add a broken yellow line down the middle of the road using simple straight stitches. Just for fun, attach a car-shaped button on the road. I used a blue button to match my car.

KEY

- A
- B
- C
- D
- E
- F
- G
- K
  Knit
- D — Duplicate Stitch
  To be done after all other knitting is complete
- V — S1
  Slip 1 purl-wise with yarn in back
- / — K2tog
  Knit 2 together
- No stitch
  Note: The "no stitch" squares are placeholders for stitches that are gained or lost throughout the design. *Do not skip a stitch.* Simply treat these squares as if they do not exist.
- • — P
  Purl
- / — P2tog
  Purl 2 together

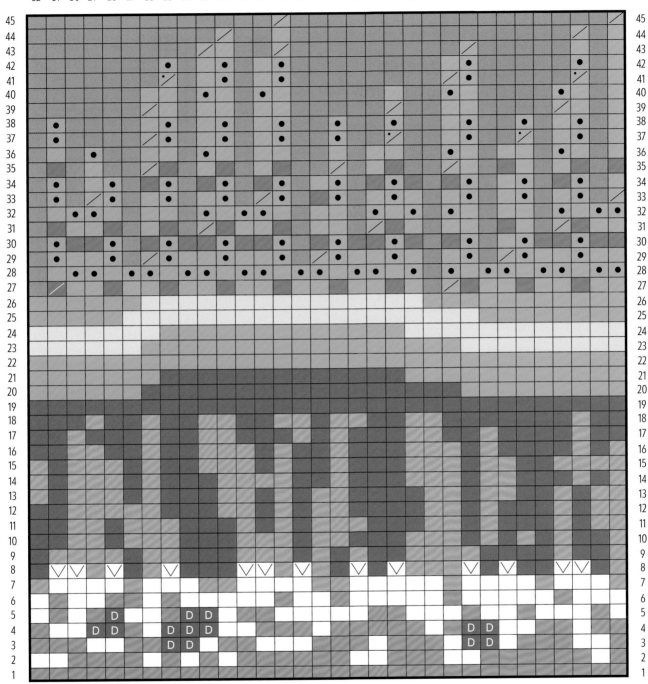

D Knit this stitch in color A,
   duplicate stitch in color D

Monarchs of the Central Coast

With their iconic orange-and-black wing patterns, monarchs are one of the most beloved and recognized butterflies in all of North America. Scientists study them, conservationists protect them, and young children can't help but chase them! Depending on where you live and the time of year, monarchs can be found in parks, nature centers, butterfly sanctuaries, and many other (sometimes unexpected) places. But, spotting one in your own backyard is simply magical. I'm watching one out of the window as I write this!

The monarch metamorphosis from egg to caterpillar to chrysalis to butterfly makes for a perfect early biology lesson for students. But, their predictable seasonal migration patterns are particularly fascinating, especially because they are the only butterflies known to make a two-way migration! Just like many other animals around the world, monarchs instinctively know when it's time to head for warmer climates. Some groups travel up to 3,000 miles / 4,830 km, pollinating plants and flowers along the way. Definitely a very important part of their journey!

Monarchs east of the Rocky Mountains from the U.S. and Canada overwinter in Mexico, while monarchs west of the Rockies head to several locations along the central coast of California. The greatest numbers are found in Pismo Beach and the quaint seaside town of Pacific Grove (also known as Butterfly Town, USA). To the delight of locals and tourists alike, thousands of monarchs gather each fall in the protected groves of Monterey pines and eucalyptus trees until it's time to head north again when the temperatures rise in early spring. The residents of Pacific Grove embrace their long history with butterflies all year, but the celebration really kicks up every fall with a Butterfly Days Festival and Parade. After the food, music, contests, and crafts are over, a visit to the butterfly sanctuary provides an up-close view of the stars of the show— the beautiful monarch butterflies clinging to tree branches in clusters. The brownish color of the closed wings blends in with the branches, but their brilliant orange is exposed as they open their wings to warm in the sun and begin fluttering overhead. The sight is unforgettable.

Inspired by the unmistakable colors and wing patterns of this amazing butterfly, this beautiful beanie features simple stranded colorwork with a touch of duplicate stitching. Show your love of monarchs (and all butterflies) with this bold design that's fun to knit and fun to wear. Try it in a variety of different colors to represent your other favorite butterflies— or even the ones in your own imagination.

SIZE

One size fits an average adult size head (approx. 19 in. / 48 cm to 22 in. / 56 cm). Finished circumference: approx. 20¼ in. / 51.5 cm.

YARN

Worsted weight yarn (#4) in four colors. Shown in:

- **A:** Stunning String Studio Legacy Worsted: Little Black Dress (50 g / 108 yd. / 99 m)
- **B:** Malabrigo, Rios: Natural (10 g / 21 yd. / 19 m)
- **C:** Malabrigo Rios: Sunset (10 g / 21 yd. / 19 m)
- **D:** Peekaboo Yarns Merino Worsted: Orange Blaze (25 g / 54 yd. / 49 m)

NEEDLES

- US size 5 / 3.75 mm, 16 in. / 40 cm circular knitting needles
- US size 7 / 4.5 mm, 16 in. / 40 cm circular knitting needles
- US size 7 / 4.5 mm set of double-pointed needles (DPNs) (or size needed to obtain gauge)

Continued on next page

KNITTING INSTRUCTIONS

With smaller circular needles and color A, cast on 96 stitches. Place single color marker and join in the round, being careful not to twist stitches.

Work (k1, p1) ribbing pattern for 1½ to 2 in. / 4 to 5 cm.

Switch to larger needles and work chart from right to left beginning on Row 1, bottom right corner. Chart repeats three times around the hat. Use remaining two stitch markers of another color to mark chart repeats.

Note: In order to avoid long "floats" (strands of yarn on the inside of the hat) and to help maintain your tension, do not carry a color more than three or four stitches without twisting the colors around each other in the back of work.

Switch to DPNs when work becomes too small for circular needles.

FINISHING

After chart is complete, cut yarn, leaving a 10 in. / 25.5 cm tail. Using a tapestry needle, weave tail through remaining stitches and pull tightly to close circle.

Pull tail to inside and weave in all ends.

Block as desired. See p. 12 for my favorite hat blocking technique.

Duplicate stitches: After all knitting and blocking is complete, work duplicate stitches where shown.

KEY

■	A
□	B
▨	C
▨	D
□	K Knit
D	Duplicate Stitch To be done after all other knitting is complete
⁄	K2tog Knit 2 together
■	No stitch **Note:** The "no stitch" squares are placeholders for stitches that are gained or lost throughout the design. *Do not skip a stitch.* Simply treat these squares as if they do not exist.
＼	SSK Slip, Slip, Knit: Slip 2 stitches knitwise, place stitches back on left needle, knit 2 tog through back loop

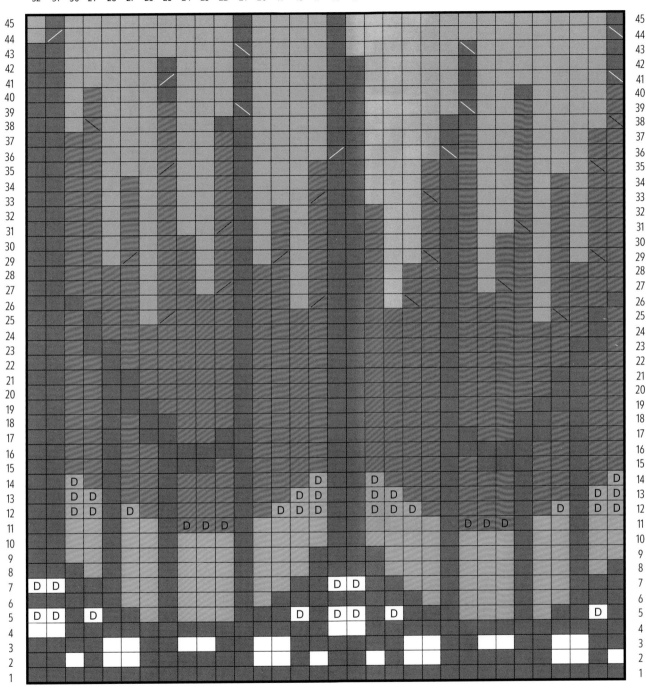

	Knit in color A, duplicate stitch in color B
D	Knit in color C, duplicate stitch in color D
D	Knit in color D, duplicate stitch in color C

Gray Whale Migration

If you've ever been on a whale-watching trip, you probably know that feeling of waiting and waiting to see a whale. The sight of sea lions and pelicans near the dock stirs the excitement of the wildlife viewing yet to come. Once out on the open water, dolphins are usually the next sighting, playfully swimming in groups right next to the boat almost as if they're wecoming you to their world. You know the main attraction can't be far off now! Still, the wait continues. You don't want to take your eyes off the water or take a break for fear of missing the magical moment. And then, the captain spots them. Whales! Cameras come out, oohs and ahhs are heard across the boat, and the whale makes its appearance! Totally worth the wait, even if it's just for a moment. Whether it's barely a glimpse of the

top of a whale, the spray from a blowhole, the flip of a tail, or a complete breach out of the water, spotting even a single whale in the wild is always exciting and memorable. They're so big!

The waters off the coast of California are like a superhighway of various whale species traveling north and south between cold arctic waters and the warmer waters of

Baja California. At various locations and at different times of year, you can spot humpbacks, orcas, and even blue whales. But the most commonly sighted is the California gray whale, some of which travel 12,000 miles / 19,300 km in one round-trip migration. Nearly every town up and down the coast offers whale-watching trips of various lengths from one- or two-hour excursions to all-day adventures. Pack up a few snacks (and possibly some ginger ale or dramamine) and it's a great family adventure or day date. The captains are knowlegable, experienced, and know the best places to go. I just love reading the log of sightings usually posted on the dock when you purchase tickets. It tells you excatly what the folks on the boat saw yesterday, last week, or even hours before. It builds the anticipation of wondering what *your* adventure will bring.

Inspired by gray whales breaching the water against the backdrop of sunset, this stranded colorwork design features just three elements—water, sky, and whales.

SIZE

One size fits an average adult size head (approx. 19 in. / 48 cm to 22 in. / 56 cm). Finished circumference: approx. 21¼ in. / 51.5 cm.

YARN

Worsted weight yarn (#4) in three colors. Shown in:

- **A:** Stunning String Studio Legacy Worsted: Big Sky (33 g / 71 yd. / 65 m)
- **B:** Western Sky Knits Merino 17 Worsted: Peppered (25 g / 46 yd. / 42 m)
- **C:** Malabrigo Rios: Peachy (20 g / 42 yd. / 39 m)

NEEDLES

- US size 5 / 3.75 mm, 16 in. / 40 cm circular knitting needles
- US size 7 / 4.5 mm, 16 in. / 40 cm circular knitting needles
- US size 7 / 4.5 mm set of double-pointed needles (DPNs) (or size needed to obtain gauge)

Continued on next page

NOTIONS

- 3 stitch markers (two of one color and one of another color)
- Tapestry needle for weaving in ends

GAUGE

With larger needles, approx. 9½ stitches = 2 in. / 5 cm in stranded stockinette stitch blocked.

Note: If you already know you are a tight knitter (or just want a larger hat), go up one or two needle sizes for both the ribbing and the body of the hat.

KNITTING INSTRUCTIONS

With smaller circular needles and color A, cast on 96 stitches. Place single color marker and join in the round, being careful not to twist stitches.

Work {k1tbl (knit through back loop), p1} ribbing pattern for 1½ to 2 in. / 4 to 5 cm.

Switch to larger needles and work chart from right to left beginning on Row 1, bottom right corner. Chart repeats three times around the hat. Use remaining two stitch markers of another color to mark chart repeats.

Note: In order to avoid long "floats" (strands of yarn on the inside of the hat) and to help maintain your tension, do not carry a color more than three or four stitches without twisting the colors around each other in the back of work.

Switch to DPNs when work becomes too small for circular needles.

FINISHING

After chart is complete, cut yarn, leaving a 10 in. / 25.5 cm tail. Using a tapestry needle, weave tail through remaining stitches and pull tightly to close circle. Pull tail to inside and weave in all ends.

Block as desired. See p. 12 for my favorite hat blocking technique.

KEY

⬛	A
⬜	B
⬜	C
⬜	K Knit
▨	K2tog Knit 2 together
⬛	No stitch

Note: The "no stitch" squares are placeholders for stitches that are gained or lost throughout the design. *Do not skip a stitch.* Simply treat these squares as if they do not exist.

Monterey Sea Life

When the entire western border of your state is more than 900 miles / 1,450 km of coastline (roughly the distance from Jackson, Florida, to New York City), the ocean and everything about it becomes an important part of who you are, and . . . you're going to have a *lot* of sea life! From San Diego to the coast of Northern California, you'll find aquariums, oceanography institutes, piers, cruise ship terminals, shipping yards, and, of course, dozens and dozens of marinas. Everything that helps us connect with, learn about, or simply enjoy the ocean and its inhabitants can be found along the coast.

Exploring tidepools and looking for seashells are great opportunities for families to learn important lessons about sea creatures, such as what's okay to pick up and what's not. Sometimes it's easy to forget that the pretty shell you just found could be someone's home, until you see it walking away! Harbor cruises and whale-watching tours take us a bit closer to dolphins, sea lions, otters, and whales. Interested in elephant seals? Stop at an overlook along the central coast near San Simeon for a view of hundreds of these huge marine mammals on the beach. They gather for mating, birthing, molting, and resting. No matter the season, the sights and sounds of so many elephant seals in one place is spectacular! One of the most rewarding opportunities for viewing and learning about sea life *up close* is by visiting an aquarium. You'll find several all up and down the coast, but one of the most famous is the Monterey Bay Aquarium. Perched right on the edge of the southern end of Monterey Bay in Cannery Row, the aquarium exhibits include sea jellies, sharks, deep sea creatures, tuna, and so much more, including an underwater view of a kelp forest teeming with sea life. Aside from the aquarium, Monterey Bay itself is a Pacific Coast gem. From Pacific Grove through Cannery Row and Fisherman's Wharf, you'll find classic oceanfront shops, restaurants, hotels, and all the saltwater taffy and clam chowder you can eat. Prior to our last road trip to the bay, we watched the movie *Cannery Row*, because the story was set in Monterey. It was fun to recognize a few spots from the movie and to compare Steinbeck's view of the area to what it is today. Farther north, the coast is lined with state beaches before reaching Santa Cruz and the California redwoods.

This design was inspired by the abundant sea life of Monterey Bay. Bright orange garibaldi (the state fish of California) and schools of sardines swim among a kelp forest in the brilliant blue sea.

SIZE

One size fits an average adult size head (approx. 19 in. / 48 cm to 22 in. / 56 cm). Finished circumference: approx. 20¼ in. / 51.5 cm.

YARN

Worsted weight yarn (#4) in four colors. Shown in:

- **A:** Peekaboo Yarns Merino Worsted: Kiwi (20 g / 44 yd. / 40 m)
- **B:** Lazer Sheep Yarns Worsted Superwash: I Speak Sheep (50 g / 100 yd. / 91 m)
- **C:** Anzula Luxury Fibers For Better or Worsted: Arizona (10 g / 20 yd. / 18 m)
- **D:** Peekaboo Yarns Merino Worsted: Classic Silver (10 g / 22 yd./ 20 m)

NEEDLES

- US size 5 / 3.75 mm, 16 in. / 40 cm circular knitting needles
- US size 7 / 4.5 mm, 16 in. / 40 cm circular knitting needles
- US size 7 / 4.5 mm set of double-pointed needles (DPNs) (or size needed to obtain gauge)

Continued on next page

NOTIONS

- 3 stitch markers (two of one color and one of another color)
- Tapestry needle for weaving in ends and working duplicate stitches

GAUGE

With larger needles, approx. 9½ stitches = 2 in. / 5 cm in stranded stockinette stitchb blocked.

Note: If you already know you are a tight knitter (or just want a larger hat), go up one or two needle sizes for both the ribbing and the body of the hat.

KNITTING INSTRUCTIONS

With smaller circular needles and color A, cast on 96 stitches. Place single color marker and join in the round, being careful not to twist stitches.

Work (k1, p1) ribbing pattern for 1½ to 2 in. / 4 to 5 cm.

Switch to larger needles and work chart from right to left beginning on Row 1, bottom right corner. Chart repeats three times around the hat. Use remaining two stitch markers of another color to mark chart repeats.

Note: In order to avoid long "floats" (strands of yarn on the inside of the hat) and to help maintain your tension, do not carry a color more than three or four stitches without twisting the colors around each other in the back of work.

Switch to DPNs when work becomes too small for circular needles.

FINISHING

After chart is complete, cut yarn, leaving a 10 in. / 25.5 cm tail. Using a tapestry needle, weave tail through remaining stitches and pull tightly to close circle. Pull tail to inside and weave in all ends.

Block as desired. See p. 12 for my favorite hat blocking technique.

Duplicate stitches: After all other knitting and blocking is complete, work duplicate stitches where shown.

KEY

▨	A
▨	B
▨	C
☐	D
☐	K Knit
D	Duplicate Stitch To be done after all other knitting is complete
▽	S1 Slip 1 purl-wise with yarn in back
╱	K2tog Knit 2 together
■	No stitch **Note:** The "no stitch" squares are placeholders for stitches that are gained or lost throughout the design. *Do not skip a stitch.* Simply treat these squares as if they do not exist.
▽²	Kfb Knit in front and back of next stitch
⋉⋊	LC Left Crossover: With yarn in front, slip 1 stitch purlwise, p1, wrap yarn over needle from back to front, pass the slipped st over the p1 and the wrap and then off the needle.

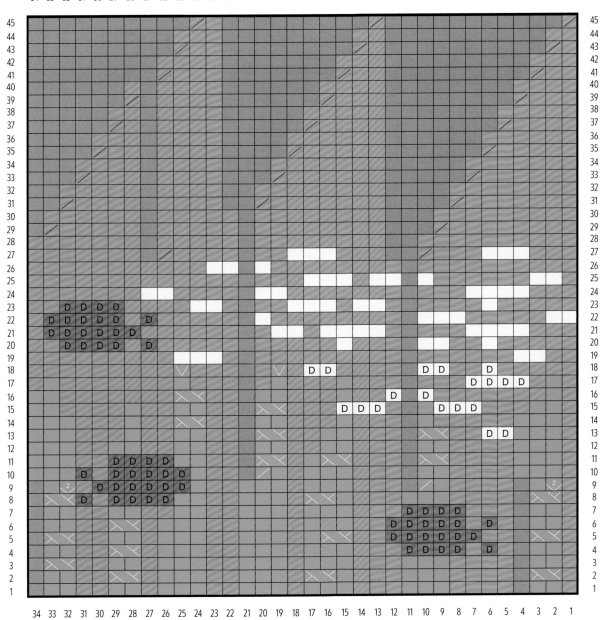

D Knit these stitches in colors A or B (depending on where they are
in the chart), duplicate stitch in color C

D Knit these stitches in color B , duplicate stitch in color D

NORTHERN
CALIFORNIA

Golden Gate Fog

The Golden Gate Bridge in San Francisco is one of the most recognizable man-made structures in the world. Just as the Statue of Liberty is a symbol of the East Coast, the Golden Gate Bridge is a symbol of the West. Whether it's in movies, television, or advertising, just one glimpse of the reddish-orange suspension bridge across a foggy bay and you know—it's California. Construction of this engineering masterpiece began in 1933 and was completed in 1937. The physics involved in the planning and the difficulty of building such a massive structure are simply mind-boggling. And it's still going strong!!

Every time we drive to San Francisco, the excitement of seeing the bridge in the distance and watching it get closer and closer is still exciting. No matter how many times we cross it, I can't help but take photos along the way—every time! My favorite memory of the Golden Gate Bridge is from the time we walked across it. The bridge is 1.7 miles / 2.7 km across, which means a round trip of about 3.5 miles / 5.6 km. But so worth it. At first, the close proximity of the traffic seems a little scary, but the sidewalk is elevated a bit and is separated by a very sturdy-looking fence. Once you get about halfway across, it starts feeling windier and colder, but the views of the city and the bay (including famous Alcatraz Island) are spectacular. It's even more interesting if a large boat passes underneath. Once you reach the other side, simply turn around and walk back, enjoying more amazing views along the way.

On either end of the Bridge, Golden Gate National Recreation Area offers up all sorts of activities that might seem unexpected for being so close to a major city. You'll find hiking trials, visitor centers, campgrounds, historical structures, biking, birdwatching, and so much more. With the boundaries of the National Recreation Area extending north to include Marin Headlands, Muir Woods, and on up to Point Reyes, it's as if the Golden Gate Bridge not only carries travelers from one side of the bay to the other, but it also transports them from the bustling city to the great outdoors.

The bold color and iconic shape of the Golden Gate take center stage in this design with the subtle outlines of hills and the city in the background. Alpaca yarn adds a bit of haziness to the fog just rolling into the bay at sunrise.

SIZE

One size fits an average adult size head (approx. 19 in. / 48 cm to 22 in. / 56 cm). Finished circumference: approx. 20¼ in. / 51.5 cm.

YARN

Worsted weight yarn (#4) in six colors. Shown in:

☐ **A:** Malabrigo Rios: Natural (20 g / 42 yd. / 39 m) held together throughout with Lana Grossa Silkhair: White (5 g / 42 yd. / 39 m) (one strand of each)

◼ **B:** Stunning String Studio Legacy Worsted: Big Sky (10 g / 22 yd. / 20 m)

◼ **C:** LL Yarn Co LL Worsted: Marmalade (20 g / 45 yd. / 41 m)

◼ **D:** Stunning String Studio Legacy Worsted: Stone (10 g / 22 yd. / 20 m)

☐ **E:** Peekaboo Yarns Merino Worsted: Classic Silver (10 g / 22 yd. / 20 m)

◻ **F:** Malabrigo Rios: Peachy (20 g / 42 yd. / 39 m)

Note: For color A I chose to use a strand of fingering weight mohair *along with* the worsted weight to create a "foggy" appearance. To keep the ribbing from being too large, I went down to size 4 needles for the *ribbing only* (not for the first few rows of the hat). If you are using worsted weight alone for the ribbing, use size 5 as listed.

Continued on next page

NEEDLES

- US size 5 / 3.75 mm, 16 in. / 40 cm circular knitting needles (or size 4; see note above)
- US size 7 / 4.5 mm, 16 in. / 40 cm circular knitting needles
- US size 7 / 4.5 mm set of double-pointed needles (DPNs) (or size needed to obtain gauge)

NOTIONS

- 3 stitch markers (two of one color and one of another color)
- Tapestry needle for weaving in ends and working duplicate stitches

GAUGE

With larger needles, approx. 9½ stitches = 2 in. / 5 cm in stranded stockinette stitch blocked.

Note: If you already know you are a tight knitter (or just want a larger hat), go up one or two needle sizes for both the ribbing and the body of the hat.

KNITTING INSTRUCTIONS

With smaller circular needles and color A, cast on 96 stitches. Place single color marker and join in the round, being careful not to twist stitches.

Work (k1, p1) ribbing pattern for 1½ to 2 in / 4 to 5 cm.

Switch to larger needles and work chart from right to left beginning on Row 1, bottom right corner. Chart repeats three times around the hat. Use remaining two stitch markers of another color to mark chart repeats.

Note: In order to avoid long "floats" (strands of yarn on the inside of the hat) and to help maintain your tension, do not carry a color more than three or four stitches without twisting the colors around each other in the back of work.

Switch to DPNs when work becomes too small for circular needles.

FINISHING

After chart is complete, cut yarn, leaving a 10 in. / 25.5 cm tail. Using a tapestry needle, weave tail through remaining stitches and pull tightly to close circle. Pull tail to inside and weave in all ends.

Block as desired. See p. 12 for my favorite hat blocking technique.

Work duplicate stitches where shown.

KEY

☐	A
◼	B
◼	C
◼	D
☐	E
▨	F
☐	K Knit
D	Duplicate Stitch To be done after all other knitting is complete
V	S1 Slip 1 purl-wise with yarn in back
/	K2tog Knit 2 together
◼	No stitch **Note:** The "no stitch" squares are placeholders for stitches that are gained or lost throughout the design. *Do not skip a stitch.* Simply treat these squares as if they do not exist.

32 31 30 29 28 27 26 25 24 23 22 21 20 19 18 17 16 15 14 13 12 11 10 9 8 7 6 5 4 3 2 1
45 44 43 42 41 40 39 38 37 36 35 34 33 32 31 30 29 28 27 26 25 24 23 22 21 20 19 18 17 16 15 14 13 12 11 10 9 8 7 6 5 4 3 2 1
D
D
D

California State Flag

A bear named Monarch, an immigrant from Norway, famous family names, and a twenty-five-day uprising. What do these things have in common? They're all part of the fascinating history of the California State Flag—the Bear Flag!

On June 14, 1846, a small group of American settlers marched upon the Mexican-run barracks in Sonoma, raised a homemade flag with a bear on it, and declared California a republic, independent from Mexico. Although no shots were fired and no one was injured, the incident came to be known as the Bear Flag Revolt or the Bear Flag Uprising. This new flag flew over the barracks for less than a month before Navy Lieutenant Joseph Warren Revere (grandson of Paul Revere) replaced it with the Stars and Stripes on July 9.

It's believed the first Bear Flag was made by Peter Storm (an immigrant from Norway) but was quickly replaced by another bear flag created by William L. Todd (a relative of Mary Todd Lincoln). Some historians believe both original flags were destroyed in the fires of the 1906 San Francisco earthquake. Others believe Storm kept his flag for the remainder of his life and that it is buried with him.

The California grizzly bear (extinct since the 1920s) was chosen for the flag as a symbol of great strength. The star represents sovereignty, the red signifies courage, and the white stands for purity. The Bear Flag was officially adopted as the state flag in 1911. The bear image at the time was inspired by Monarch, the last California grizzly bear in captivity in the San Francisco Zoo. After several revisions, the final version of the flag was adopted in 1953. History buffs can still step back in time and visit the original barracks at lovely Sonoma State Historic Park or check out Bear Flag Monument in Sonoma Plaza and stand at the very site where the first Bear Flag was flown!

My favorite part of the flag has always been the bear. Although California grizzly bears no longer roam the mountains and foothills of the state, we do have lots of black bears. I've seen them many times in Sequoia National Park, which is always exciting, but a little scary (depending on how close the bear is).

This design features a fun adaptation of the state flag (and a big fat bear) against a clear blue sky with an optional pompom of golden sunshine. Leave the finished hat as is or add simple embroidered words, such as CALIFORNIA, CALIFORNIA REPUBLIC, or I ❤ CALIFORNIA. The choice is yours!

SIZE

One size fits an average adult size head (approx. 19 in. / 48 cm to 22 in. / 56 cm). Finished circumference: approx. 21¼ in. / 54 cm.

YARN

Worsted weight yarn (#4) in five (or seven) colors. Shown in:

- **A:** Aly Bee Workshop Merino Worsted Festive (20 g / 40 yd. / 37 m)
- **B:** Aly Bee Workshop Merino Worsted Cindersnap (10 g / 20 yd. / 18 m)
- **C:** Aly Bee Workshop Merino Worsted Cold Brew (20 g / 40 yd. / 37 m)
- **D:** Malabrigo, Rios: Natural (25 g / 53 yd. / 48 m)
- **E:** Aly Bee Workshop Merino Worsted Glass Slipper (20 g / 40 yd. / 37 m)

Optional: Any bright yellow yarn for the pom-pom (I used Goldenrod from Stunning String Studios) and a few yards of black for embroidering the words

NEEDLES

- US size 5 / 3.75 mm, 16 in. / 40 cm circular knitting needles
- US size 7 / 4.5 mm, 16 in. / 40 cm circular knitting needles
- US size 7 / 4.5 mm set of double-pointed needles (DPNs) (or size needed to obtain gauge)

Continued on next page

NOTIONS

- 3 stitch markers (two of one color and one of another color)
- Tapestry needle for weaving in ends and working embroidery

GAUGE

With larger needles, approx. 9 ½ stitches = 2 in. / 5 cm in stranded stockinette stitch blocked.

Note: If you already know you are a tight knitter (or just want a larger hat), go up one or two needle sizes for both the ribbing and the body of the hat.

KNITTING INSTRUCTIONS

With smaller circular needles and color A, cast on 96 stitches. Place single color marker and join in the round, being careful not to twist, stitches.

Work (k1, p1) ribbing pattern for 1½ to 2 in. / 4 to 5 cm.

Switch to larger needles and work chart from right to left beginning on Row 1, bottom right corner. Chart repeats three times around the hat. Use remaining two stitch markers of another color to mark chart repeats.

Note: In order to avoid long

"floats" (strands of yarn on the inside of the hat) and to help maintain your tension, do not carry a color more than three or four stitches without twisting the colors around each other in the back of work. To help keep tension even, be sure to spread out your stitches on the right needle about every four stitches.

Switch to DPNs when work becomes too small for circular needles.

FINISHING

After chart is complete, cut yarn, leaving a 10 in. / 25.5 cm tail. Using a tapestry needle, weave tail through remaining stitches and pull tightly to close circle. Pull tail to inside and weave in all ends.

Block as desired. See p. 12 for my favorite hat blocking technique.

Embroidery: After all knitting and blocking is complete, add embroidered stars as shown in the photo using Festive (color A). See Figure 1 for star embroidery guidelines.

Optional: Using your favorite method, make a bright yellow pom-pom and attach to top of hat.

Optional: Add embroidered

words as shown in the photo. Use Figure 2, 3, or 4 to add CALIFORNIA or I ❤ CALIFORNIA (or leave blank for no words at all). To help with placement of words on your hat, the small blue arrow on each figure marks the center.

KEY

■	A
▦	B
■	C
□	D
▨	E
□	K Knit
◪	K2tog Knit 2 together
■	No stitch

Note: The "no stitch" squares are placeholders for stitches that are gained or lost throughout the design. *Do not skip a stitch.* Simply treat these squares as if they do not exist.

Fig. 1

Fig. 2

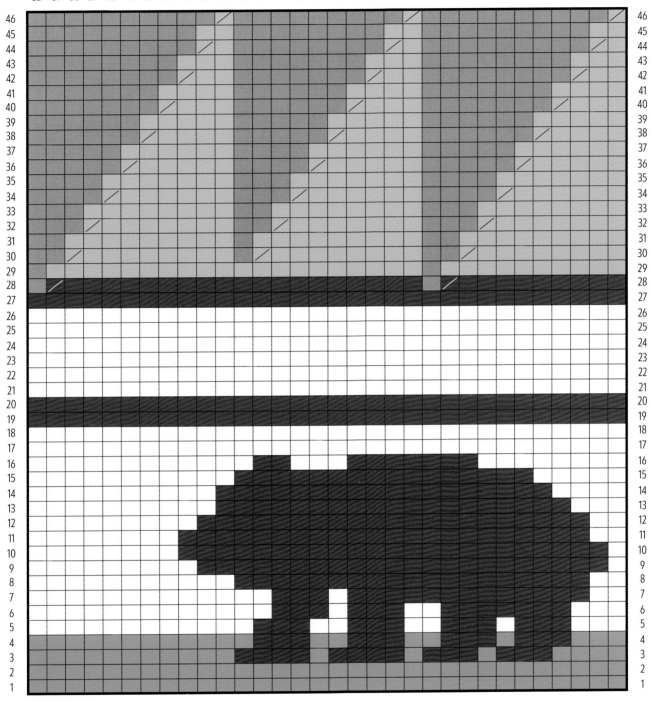

Fig. 3

Wine Country

California is home to four main wine-producing regions: South Coast, Central Valley, Central Coast, and North Coast . . . including hundreds of places in between and all around! At last count, more than 4,300 wineries were in operation across the state, many of which produce some of the finest wines in the world. Not bad for an area that's been growing grapes for less than 260 years.

The ups and downs of the California wine industry began in 1769 when the first vines were planted at the San Diego mission. By the time the gold rush was in full swing, the demand for wine skyrocketed, and many vineyards were established in Northern California, mainly in the Napa Valley region. The Prohibition years of the 1920s nearly destroyed

the commercial wine industry. Even after Prohibition was repealed, it took more than fifty years for the industry to recover. A pivotal turn came in 1976 when several California wines went head-to-head with French wines in a blind taste test and came out the winners! Although amazing wines are produced throughout the state, Napa Valley remains at the heart of wine country.

Today's wineries in Napa, Sonoma, and the surrounding areas encompass so much more than simply wine tasting. They have become vacation destinations, wedding venues, and honeymoon spots. Wineries run the gamut from upscale and sophisticated with fine dining, spa facilities, and 5-star accommodations to casual cowboy vibes with rustic settings, picnics, and bonfire barbecues. You can ride bikes through vineyards, take a tour, listen to live music, sample olive oils and craft cheeses, and even ride a vintage train. At the right time of year, you can join in the harvest with stomping parties and celebrations. There's truly something for everybody. The rolling hillsides covered with vineyards and the countryside itself is so spectacularly beautiful that even a drive from winery to winery is a great getaway. We recently visited in autumn and were surprised to see the fall colors not only in the trees surrounding the wineries but also in the vineyards themselves. Many of the grape leaves had turned orange or yellow. So pretty! I'd love to see them in winter.

In three rich colors of wine, vines, and trellises, this fun yet sophisticated design brings the spirit of California's wine country to knitting. The main body showcases a fun crossover stitch that creates the look of wooden arbors and trellises covered in vines. A band of wine-colored stockinette stitch with mini bobble grape clusters adds just a touch of whimsy and understated diagonal textured rows represent the vineyards on the hillsides.

SIZE

One size fits an average adult size head (approx. 19 in. / 48 cm to 22 in. / 56 cm). Finished circumference: approx. 20¼ in. / 51.5 cm.

YARN

Worsted weight yarn (#4) in three colors. Shown in:

- **A:** Stunning String Studio Legacy Worsted: Mulled Wine (25 g / 54 yd. / 49 m)
- **B:** Aly Bee Workshop Merino Worsted: Cold Brew (20 g / 40 yd. / 37 m)
- **C:** Stunning String Studio Legacy Worsted: Black Forest (33 g / 71 yd. / 65 m)

NEEDLES

- US size 5 / 3.75 mm, 16 in. / 40 cm circular knitting needles
- US size 7 / 4.5 mm, 16 in. / 40 cm circular knitting needles
- US size 7 / 4.5 mm set of double-pointed needles (DPNs) (or size needed to obtain gauge)

NOTIONS

- 4 stitch markers (three of one color and one of another color)
- Tapestry needle for weaving in ends

Continued on next page

GAUGE

With larger needles, approx. 9½ stitches = 2 in. / 5 cm in stranded stockinette stitch blocked.

Note: If you already know you are a tight knitter (or just want a larger hat), go up one or two needle sizes for both the ribbing and the body of the hat.

KNITTING INSTRUCTIONS

With smaller circular needles and color A, cast on 96 stitches. Place single color marker and join in the round, being careful not to twist stitches.

Work (k2, p2) ribbing pattern for 1½ to 2 in. / 4 to 5 cm.

Switch to larger needles and work chart from right to left beginning on Row 1, bottom right corner. Chart repeats four times around the hat. Use remaining three stitch markers of another color to mark chart repeats.

Note: The first three rows contain several "no stitch" squares. Treat these stitches as if they don't exist, which means the first three rows are simply knit all around.

Switch to DPNs when work becomes too small for circular needles.

Note: There is no stranded colorwork in this design. Each row is worked using only one color. In Rows 5 to 7, 10 to 12, and 15 to 17, you will knit with color C and simply slip color B.

FINISHING

After chart is complete, cut yarn, leaving a 10 in. / 25.5 cm tail. Using a tapestry needle, weave tail through remaining stitches and pull tightly to close circle. Pull tail to inside and weave in all ends.

Block as desired. See p. 12 for my favorite hat blocking technique.

KEY

▨	A
▨	B
▨	C
☐	K Knit
☑	S1 Slip 1 purl-wise with yarn in back
⧄	K2tog Knit 2 together
▧	No stitch **Note:** The "no stitch" squares are placeholders for stitches that are gained or lost throughout the design. *Do not skip a stitch.* Simply treat these squares as if they do not exist.
⊡	P Purl
⬤	Mb Make Bobble: (P1, k1, p1, k1) into next stitch, then lift 2nd, 3rd, and 4th stitches over first stitch and off needle, one at a time
◯	YO² Double Wrap Yarn Over: In this design, all yarn overs are double wrapped to create long loops

⊠ Crossover Stitch Drop first long loop off needle, slip 3 stitches purlwise to right needle, drop 2nd long loop. With left needle, pick up the first long loop, pass 3 slipped stitches back to left needle, then pick up the 2nd long loop and place on left needle. K5 (you'll be knitting a long loop, 3 stitches in between, and a second long loop).

⧄	K3tog Knit 3 together
⧄	P2tog Purl 2 together

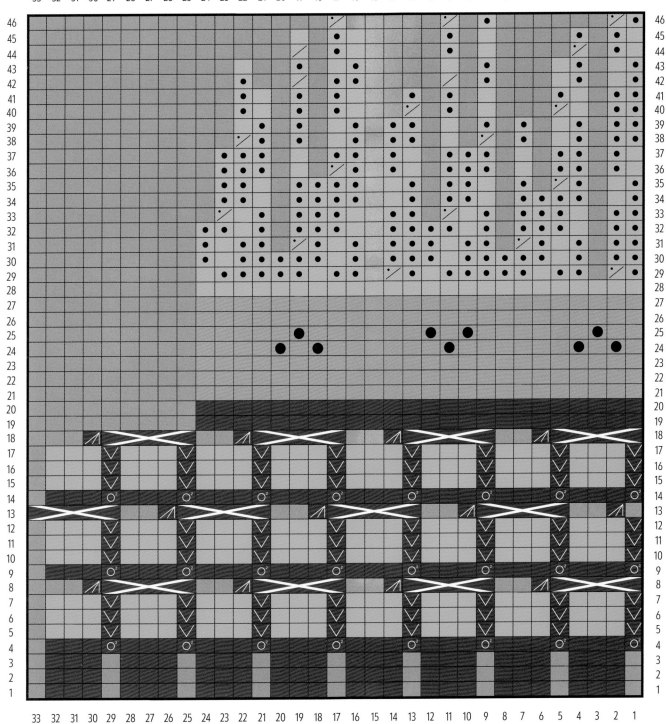

Special instructions for Rows 12, 13, and 14: Work Row 12 as shown. Before beginning Row 13 (and at beginning of each chart repeat in this round), remove marker, slip long loop to right needle, replace marker, and continue knitting round as shown. After Row 13 is complete, move markers back to original locations as you knit Row 14. Knit remainder of chart as shown.

The Lumberjack

Where you find forests, you'll likely find lumberjacks (at some point in history, anyway). For centuries, humans have used the resources around them to provide shelter, boats, and other necessities for their families, including wood for fuel. In the decades following the gold rush in California, the demand for lumber grew exponentially and went far beyond the needs of one's own family. Lumberjacks (the people who were paid to cut down trees) worked day after day to keep up with the growth in the logging industry. Over time, many of the now protected groves of redwoods, sequoias, and other forests were nearly wiped out. Fortunately, enough foresighted folks worked to put a stop to it. Because of the unplanned and unsustainable logging practices of the past, the

logging industry in California today is a fraction of what it once was. Today's loggers (in California and beyond) are much more concientious in their approach toward harvesting this valuable and renewable resouce. Still, the spirit of the old-timey lumberjack lives on in folktales, songs, plays, and even modern-day competitions.

The work of a lumberjack took a great deal of strength, skill, endurance, and even courage. Imagine working around falling trees and rolling logs. It was a dangerous occupation! In the early days, *all* of the work relied on hand tools and muscle. Over time, it was natural for lumberjacks to eventually become competitive in their show of strength and speed. Today, in professional and amateur lumberjack competitions around the country (and around the world), men and women compete in contests such as logrolling, speed climbing, log cutting, and axe throwing. That same show of strength, skill, and endurance that was once a necessity is now a competitive sport and a source of entertainment. How fun! The names of top competitors become famous in the world of lumberjacks, just as the names of the strongest lumberjacks of the past spread in the logging camps. But, by far, the most famous lumberjack of all time was Paul Bunyan, the flannel-wearing, larger-than-life, tall-tale hero who could clear an entire forest with one swing of his axe! This beloved folktale character has become the symbol of lumberjacks everywhere. Statues of Paul and his companion, Babe the Blue Ox, can be spotted from Maine to the coast of California, where you'll find one of the tallest Pauls of all near Redwood National and State Parks.

Red plaid or checkered flannel shirts are the unofficial and universally recognized "uniform" of lumberjacks and the inspiration for this design. As a huge fan of flannel shirts, I jumped at the chance to represent the lumberjacks of Northern California with this buffalo-check pattern turned plaid using a crochet hook method to add vertical stripes. A few wooden buttons add to the look of a flannel shirt.

SIZE

One size fits an average adult size head (approx. 19 in. / 48 cm to 22 in. / 56 cm). Finished circumference: approx. 19½ in. / 49.5 cm.

YARN

DK weight yarn (#3) in three colors. Shown in Urth Yarns Harvest DK in the following colors:

- **A:** Thuja (33 g / 99 yd. / 90 m)
- **B:** Rubia (25 g / 75 yd. / 69 m)
- ☐ **C:** Thyme (20 g / 60 yd. / 55 m)

NEEDLES

- US size 4 / 3.5 mm, 16 in. / 40 cm circular knitting needles
- US size 7 / 4.5 mm, 16 in. / 40 cm circular knitting needles
- US size 7 / 4.5 mm set of double-pointed needles (DPNs) (or size needed to obtain gauge)

NOTIONS

- 3 stitch markers (two of one color and one of another color)
- Tapestry needle for weaving in ends
- Crochet hook for adding vertical stripes after knitting is complete. Choose one that is approx. the same size as your larger needle. I used size H-8 / 5 mm.
- Optional: 3 or 4 buttons (approx. ⅝ in. / 1.5 cm))
- Optional: Sewing needle and thread in a complementary color for sewing on buttons

Continued on next page

KNITTING INSTRUCTIONS

With smaller circular needles and color A, cast on 104 stitches. Place single color marker and join in the round, being careful not to twist stitches.

Work in (k1, p1) ribbing pattern for 1½ to 2 in. / 4 to 5 cm.

Increase Round: *K25, k in front and back of next stitch (kfb); repeat from * three more times—108 stitches total.

Switch to larger needles and work chart from right to left beginning on Row 1, bottom right corner. Chart repeats three times around the hat. Use remaining two stitch markers of another color to mark chart repeats.

Note: In order to avoid long "floats" (strands of yarn on the inside of the hat) and to help maintain your tension, do not carry a color more than three or four stitches without twisting the colors around each other in the back of work.

Switch to DPNs when work becomes too small for circular needles.

FINISHING

After chart is complete, cut yarn, leaving a 10 in. / 25.5 cm tail. Using a tapestry needle, weave tail through remaining stitches and pull tightly to close circle. Pull tail to inside and weave in all ends.

Vertical Stripes: Before blocking, you'll need to add the vertical stripes to complete the look of plaid. The stripes will be added in the small channels that were created with the vertical columns of purl stitches. With a crochet hook, you will essentially be working a column of chain stitches up each channel. Weave in all ends from colors A and B first, making sure to stay within the purl stitch channel. Keep your tension even.

1. Using color C and crochet hook, start at the bottom stitch of one channel. Insert hook from front to back and bring up a loop (Figure 1). Be sure to leave a tail of this color to weave in later.
2. With loop on hook, go up one stitch in the column, insert hook from front to back again and bring up another loop, pulling it through the first one (Figure 2). Hint: Make sure you are pulling loops from the working yarn and not the tail. Keeping one hand inside the hat to help guide the yarn is helpful.
3. Repeat step 2 all the way to the top of where the checkerboard pattern ends. If desired, work the lines to the top of the hat.
4. On the last loop, cut yarn, leaving an 8 to 10 in. / 20 to 25.5 cm tail, and pull through to front (Figure 3).
5. Insert crochet hook from back to front. Bring tail over the top of last loop and pull through to back to anchor in place (Figure 4).
6. Weave in all ends to inside of hat.

Block as desired. See p. 12 for my favorite hat blocking technique.

Optional: Sew on 3 or 4 buttons using yarn or regular thread. See the photo for placement suggestion.

KEY

■	A
■	B
☐	C
☐	K Knit
◿	K2tog Knit 2 together
■	No stitch **Note:** The "no stitch" squares are placeholders for stitches that are gained or lost throughout the design. *Do not skip a stitch.* Simply treat these squares as if they do not exist.
⊡	P Purl
◿	P2tog Purl 2 together
◺	SSK Slip, Slip, Knit: Slip 2 stitches knitwise, place stitches back on left needle, knit 2 tog through back loop

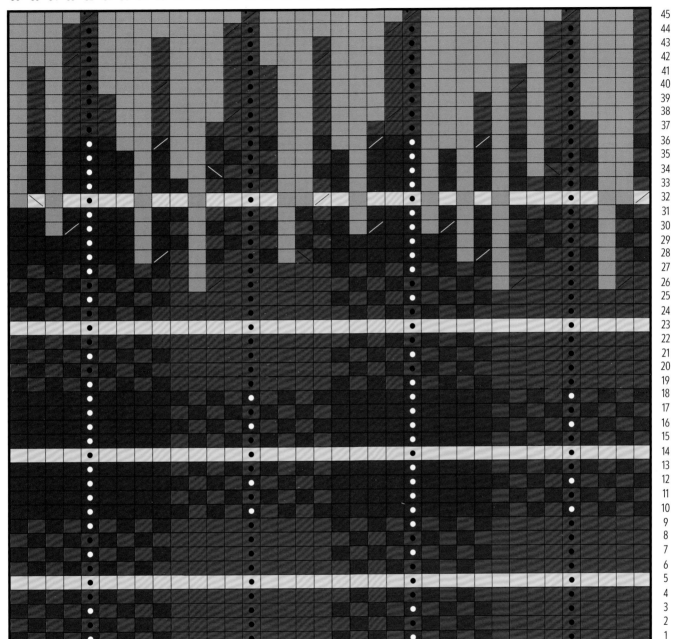

Fig. 1   Fig. 2   Fig. 3   Fig. 4

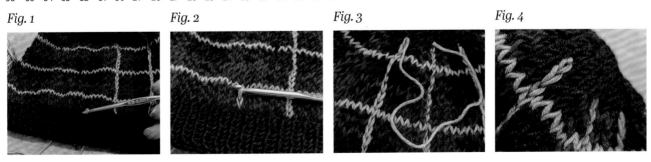

Forests of the North

From the coastal redwoods in the west to the ponderosa pines in the east, almost the entire northern section of California is covered in forests—border to border. The region is home to two national parks (Redwood and Lassen Volcanic), about a dozen state parks, numerous wilderness areas, more than twenty (active, inactive, or extinct) volcanoes, and an abundance of lakes and waterfalls. Various mountain peaks pop in and out of view as you drive through the area along Interstate 5 (the most used north/south route for travelers), but it's snowcapped Mount Shasta that stands out among the rest and dominates the landscape. On a clear day, this 14,179-foot / 4,322 m giant of a mountain (still an active volcano) can be seen from more than 100 miles / 160 km away. It's also easy to spot

from 30,000 feet / 9,144 m in the air! From the time humans first settled in the area to today, Mount Shasta has served as a landmark for navigation. You can't miss it! The scenery along the 5 is lovely, but to fully appreciate what the north has to offer, slowing down and taking a few side trips is a must. A detour in any direction could take you snowshoeing to a waterfall, exploring a cave, hiking around a volcano, or fly fishing in a river. All memorable adventures to be sure.

I recently asked my daughters what they remembered most about driving through Northern California, and they each said "lots of trees." I agree! A tree-lover at heart, I also think of trees the most. The forests of Redwood State and National Parks on the northern coast are some of my favorite places in the state. I love the creaking sound of the giant trees as they sway in the breeze and how the forest floor is filled with ferns and occasional wildflowers. The scenic drives are spectacular! Throughout the north, the sight (and scents) of Douglas fir and assorted pine trees among lakes, streams, and mountains is unforgettable. And that sound of crunching pine needles underfoot on the trail? The best!

With just a single color, this design uses a series of cable stitches and decreases to create an understated forest of pine trees around your hat. For a seasonal touch, try adding snow or even Christmas decorations to your trees using duplicate stitches, French knots, beads, or buttons.

SIZE

One size fits an average adult size head (approx. 19 in. / 48 cm to 22 in. / 56 cm). Finished circumference: approx. 19¾ in. / 51.5 cm.

YARN

Worsted weight yarn (#4) in one color. Shown in:

A: Anzula Luxury Fibers For Better or Worsted: Kale (100 g / 200 yd. / 182 m)

NEEDLES

- US size 5 / 3.75 mm, 16 in. / 40 cm circular knitting needles
- US size 7 / 4.5 mm, 16 in. / 40 cm circular knitting needles
- US size 7 / 4.5 mm set of double-pointed needles (DPNs) (or size needed to obtain gauge)

NOTIONS

- 3 stitch markers (two of one color and one of another color)
- Cable needle (cn)
- Tapestry needle for weaving in ends

GAUGE

With larger needles, approx. 9½ stitches = 2 in. / 5 cm in stranded stockinette stitch blocked.

Note: This design has a lot of cables which can sometimes cause knitting to tighten up. If you already know you are a tight knitter (or just want a larger hat), go up one or two needle sizes for both the ribbing and the body of the hat.

KNITTING INSTRUCTIONS

With smaller circular needles, cast on 96 stitches. Place single color marker and join in the round, being careful not to twist stitches.

Work the following ribbing pattern for 1½ to 2 in. / 4 to 5 cm:
Rib Pattern: *(K1, p1) 3 times, k4, (p1, k1) 3 times; repeat from * to end of round.

Switch to larger needles and work chart from right to left beginning on Row 1, bottom right corner. Chart repeats three times around the hat. Use remaining two stitch markers of another color to mark chart repeats.

Switch to DPNs when work becomes too small for circular needles.

FINISHING

After chart is complete, cut yarn, leaving a 10 in. / 25.5 cm tail. Using a tapestry needle, weave tail through remaining stitches and pull tightly to close circle. Pull tail to inside and weave in all ends.

Block as desired. See p. 12 for my favorite hat blocking technique.

KEY

	K Knit

☐ K
Knit

▱ K2tog
Knit 2 together

■ No stitch
Note: The "no stitch" squares are placeholders for stitches that are gained or lost throughout the design. *Do not skip a stitch.* Simply treat these squares as if they do not exist.

⊡ P
Purl

▱ P2tog
Purl 2 together

◩ SSK
Slip, Slip, Knit: Slip 2 stitches knitwise, place stitches back on left needle, knit 2 tog through back loop

2/2 RC
2/2 Right Cable: Slip 2 stitches to cable needle and hold in back; k2; k2 from cable needle

2/2 LC
2/2 Left Cable: Slip 2 stitches to cable needle and hold in front; k2; k2 from cable needle

1/1 LPC
1/1 Left Purl Cable: Slip 1 stitch to cable needle and hold in front; p1; k1 from cable needle

1/1 RPC
1/1 Right Purl Cable: Slip 1 stitch to cable needle and hold in back; k1; p1 from cable needle

2/1 LPC
2/1 Left Purl Cable: Slip 2 stitches to cable needle and hold in front; p1; k2 from cable needle

2/1 RPC
2/1 Right Purl Cable: Slip 1 stitch to cable needle and hold in back; k2; p1 from cable needle

1/1 RC
1/1 Right Cable: Slip 1 stitch to cable needle and hold in back; k1; k1 from cable needle

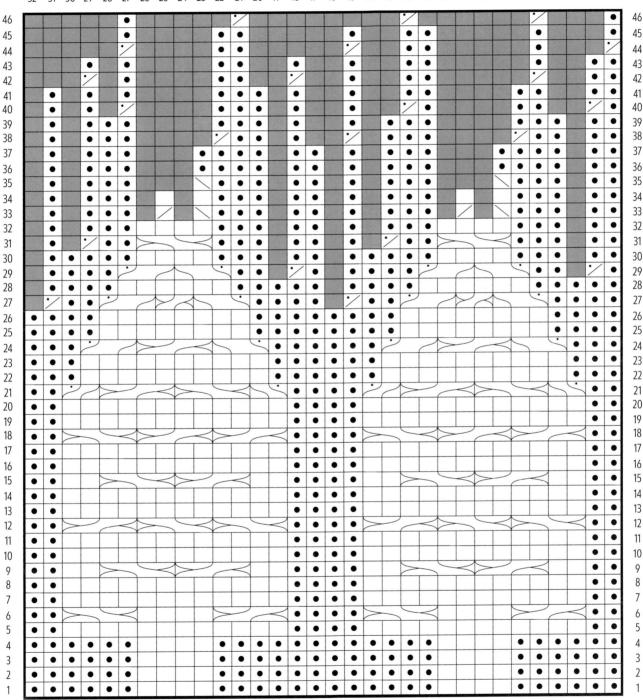

Rivers of California

If water is life, then rivers and streams are what sustains that life. Just like veins and arteries carry life-sustaining blood from our hearts to the rest of our bodies, rivers and streams carry water from snow-packed mountains and alpine lakes to the rest of the state, just as they have for centuries. Considering much of Southern California is comprised of desert, it's not surprising that most of the state's major rivers are found in the central and northern regions.

Although SoCal lacks the types of rivers that would support boating and kayaking, it does have dozens of smaller rivers and streams, including some amazing waterfalls, all fed by snowmelt from the local mountain

#2 Amy Smoker, Yurok
Miniature Trinket Basket,
1960-1970, Obsidian Blade
with Worm's Trail Design

ranges. Getting to these waterfalls makes for a variety of incredible day hikes, most of which are less than an hour away from cities.

I have many childhood memories of driving the mere thirty minutes to a small river in our local mountains where we'd swim, jump off rocks, and pretend we were famous explorers. Even the hills right behind our house had a good-size stream running through them complete with mini waterfalls tumbling over the rocks and a pond of pollywogs where the water was still. But, to see and experience major rivers (with or without rapids) you need to head north.

Each spring, the varying levels of snowpack in the Sierra Nevadas and other mountain ranges begins melting, feeding the rivers, waterfalls, streams, and lakes below in what seems a constant cylce of drought/no drought years. Aside from providing drinking water to much of the state, that water also helps trees, flowers, and farmlands flourish, provides fish to recreational and professional fishermen, and even assists the shipping idustry. While visiting Stockton (about 80 miles / 130 km inland from San Francisco Bay) last year, I was shocked to see a full-blown shipping port with huge container ships right there in town! I hadn't thought about the San Joaquin

River as being large enough for that type of transportation—but it is!

From a purely recreational standpoint, there's no shortage of opportunities for fun, adventure, and incredible sightseeing on the rivers of California—rafting on the Kern, kayaking on the Russian, tubing on the Merced, fly fishing on the Smith, cruising on the Sacramento, or simply picnicking and enjoying the view along any of them. After all, you have almost 190,000 miles / 305,775 km of rivers from which to choose!

In three distinct sections of design, this beanie begins with a fun-to-knit ripple-textured river just above the ribbing. A triangular-patterned band comes next, inspired by the neutral colors and geometric shapes found on baskets from the Yurok tribe and other indigenous people of the river regions of California. The top section features a simple basket weave.

SIZE
One size fits an average adult size head (approx. 19 in. / 48 cm to 22 in. / 56 cm). Finished circumference: approx. 20¼ in. / 51.5 cm.

YARN
Worsted weight yarn (#4) in four colors. Shown in:

- **A:** Anzula Luxury Fibers For Better or Worsted: Sexy (33 g / 66 yd. / 60 m)
- **B:** B: Anzula Luxury Fibers For Better or Worsted: Seabreeze (25 g / 50 yd. / 46 m)
- **C:** Peekaboo Yarns Merino Worsted: Warm Brown (10 g / 22 yd. / 20 m)
- **D:** Anzula Luxury Fibers For Better or Worsted: Seaside (33 g / 66 yd. / 60 m)

NEEDLES
- US size 5 / 3.75 mm, 16 in. / 40 cm circular knitting needles
- US size 7 / 4.5 mm, 16 in. / 40 cm circular knitting needles
- US size 7 / 4.5 mm set of double-pointed needles (DPNs) (or size needed to obtain gauge)

Continued on next page

NOTIONS

- 3 stitch markers (two of one color and one of another color)
- Tapestry needle for weaving in ends

GAUGE

With larger needles, approx. 9½ stitches = 2 in. / 5 cm in stranded stockinette stitch blocked.

Note: If you already know you are a tight knitter (or just want a larger hat), go up one or two needle sizes for both the ribbing and the body of the hat.

KNITTING INSTRUCTIONS

With smaller circular needles and color A, cast on 96 stitches. Place single color marker and join in the round, being careful not to twist stitches.

Work {k1tbl (knit through back loop), p1} ribbing pattern for 1½ to 2 in. / 4 to 5 cm.

Switch to larger needles and work chart from right to left beginning on Row 1, bottom right corner. Chart repeats three times around the hat. Use remaining two stitch markers of another color to mark chart repeats.

Note: In order to avoid long "floats" (strands of yarn on the inside of the hat) and to help maintain your tension, do not carry a color more than three or four stitches without twisting the colors around each other in the back of work.

Switch to DPNs when work becomes too small for circular needles.

FINISHING

After chart is complete, cut yarn, leaving a 10 in. / 25.5 cm tail.

Using a tapestry needle, weave tail through remaining stitches and pull tightly to close circle. Pull tail to inside and weave in all ends.

Block as desired. See p. 12 for my favorite hat blocking technique.

KEY

■	A
□	B
▨	C
▨	D
□	K Knit
▨	K2tog Knit 2 together
■	No stitch **Note:** The "no stitch" squares are placeholders for stitches that are gained or lost throughout the design. *Do not skip a stitch.* Simply treat these squares as if they do not exist.
⊡	P Purl
▨	P2tog Purl 2 together

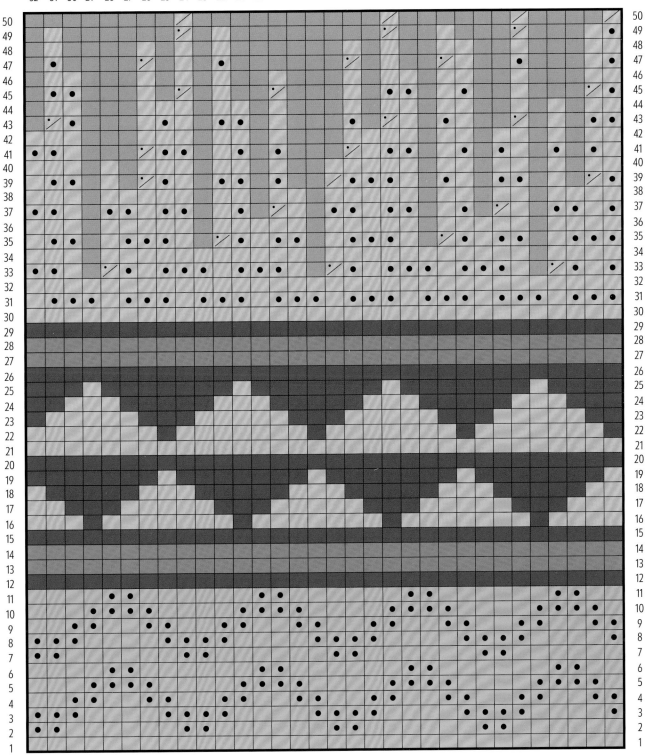

Lake Tahoe

I've been to Lake Tahoe exactly twice. The trips were only twelve years apart, but it's interesting to see how different, yet similar, the memories are. The first was a summer camping trip with my family when I was about ten years old. We had never been camping before. In the true spirit of adventure, my parents borrowed a tent and other equipment and headed to Lake Tahoe with nine kids. Arriving at the campsite after dark, my dad nearly backed the car into a tree trying to use the headlights for light as he struggled with an unfamiliar tent. We all giggled into the night, purposely rolling on top of each other in our sleeping bags, exaggerating the too-steep incline of our campsite. My sister Brenda (sleeping at the edge of the tent) swears to this day that she felt a bear lean up against her from the outside. We never found evidence, but I believe her. The next day, all of us

nine kids explored the campground, climbed on rocks, and looked for bear tracks. My younger brother (before we could stop him) suddenly scrambled to the top of a very large boulder, only to discover he couldn't get down. Our parents looked worried as I ran back to the campsite with the news "Joe's stuck on a rock!" The rest of the trip involved horseback riding with amazing views, lots of exploring, and a day of canoeing and swimming in the lake. I remember the water was so clear, you could see the rocks on the bottom even though it was deep. And I remember the trees. Everywhere! So many trees.

Fast-forward twelve years to my second Lake Tahoe trip. This time, with my husband on our autumn honeymoon. We stayed in a tiny cabin with a fireplace on the shore of the lake. I was excited to wear the sweater that I had knitted during the last few months of college, sitting under the trees between classes. The late October weather in Tahoe meant it was too cold to swim or go out on the lake at all, but I remember hiking to the water's edge and marveling at how clear the water was. And of course, I remember the trees.

Two trips in two different seasons viewed through the eyes of a child and the eyes of an adult. The summertime adventures with siblings and the cozy fall trip with just the two of us were so different, yet the overall memory of a beautiful blue lake surrounded by trees as far as you can see is exactly the same.

Lake Tahoe is the largest lake in the Sierra Nevada range, most recognizable due to its location—right at the "bend" in the state with the California/Nevada border running nearly down the center. It's known for amazing summertime activities and incredible skiing, but my favorite part of the lake is picturesque Emerald Bay State Park, a beautiful horseshoe-shaped bay with a tiny island in the middle of it.

This beanie was inspired by the view from inside Emerald Bay looking out to the tree-lined shores of the bay and across the lake to the other side with the blue sky of a summer day above. For a wintery look, try adding snow to the ground and the treetops.

SIZE

One size fits an average adult size head (approx. 19 in. / 48 cm to 22 in. / 56 cm). Finished circumference: approx. 20¼ in. / 51.5 cm.

YARN

Worsted weight yarn (#4) in five colors. Shown in:

- **A:** Stunning String Studio Legacy Worsted: Black Forest (50 g / 108 yd. / 99 m)
- **B:** Stunning String Studio Legacy Worsted: Big Sky (25 g / 54 yd. / 49 m)
- **C:** Stunning String Studio Legacy Worsted: Deep Forest (10 g / 22 yd. / 20 m)
- **D:** Malabrigo Rios: Winter Lake (10 g / 21 yd. / 19 m)
- **E:** Stunning String Studio Legacy Worsted: Cloudy Sky (10 g / 22 yd. / 20 m)

NEEDLES

- US size 5 / 3.75 mm, 16 in. / 40 cm circular knitting needles
- US size 7 / 4.5 mm, 16 in. / 40 cm circular knitting needles
- US size 7 / 4.5 mm set of double-pointed needles (DPNs) (or size needed to obtain gauge)

Continued on next page

NOTIONS

- 3 stitch markers (two of one color and one of another color)
- Tapestry needle for weaving in ends

GAUGE

With larger needles, approx. 9½ stitches = 2 in. / 5 cm in stranded stockinette stitch blocked.

Note: If you already know you are a tight knitter (or just want a larger hat) go up one or two needle sizes for both the ribbing and the body of the hat.

KNITTING INSTRUCTIONS

With smaller circular needles and color A, cast on 96 stitches. Place single color marker and join in the round, being careful not to twist stitches.

Work (k2, p2) ribbing pattern for 3½ to 4 in. / 9 to 10 cm for a double (fold-over) ribbing.

Switch to larger needles and work chart from right to left beginning on Row 1, bottom right corner. Chart repeats three times around the hat. Use remaining two stitch markers of another color to mark chart repeats.

Note: In order to avoid long "floats" (strands of yarn on the inside of the hat) and to help maintain your tension, do not carry a color more than three or four stitches without twisting the colors around each other in the back of work.

Switch to DPNs when work becomes too small for circular needles.

FINISHING

After chart is complete, cut yarn, leaving a 10 in. / 25.5 cm tail. Using a tapestry needle, weave tail through remaining stitches and pull tightly to close circle. Pull tail to inside and weave in all ends.

Block as desired. See p. 12 for my favorite hat blocking technique.

KEY

▨	A
▨	B
▨	C
▨	D
▨	E
☐	K Knit
Ⅴ	S1 Slip 1 purl-wise with yarn in back
▨	K2tog Knit 2 together
▨	No stitch **Note:** The "no stitch" squares are placeholders for stitches that are gained or lost throughout the design. *Do not skip a stitch.* Simply treat these squares as if they do not exist.
⊡	P Purl
▨	SSK Slip, Slip, Knit: Slip 2 stitches knitwise, place stitches back on left needle, knit 2 tog through back loop

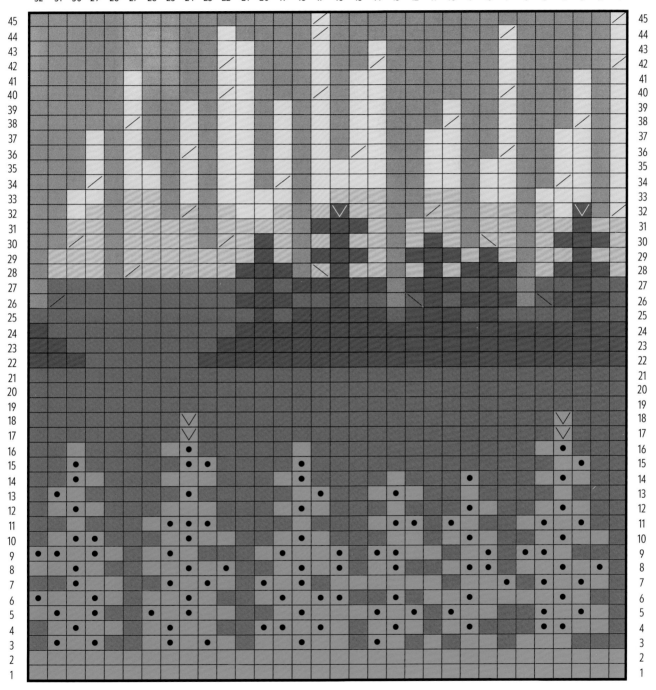

BEANIES IN THE WILD

Amber in Hollywood

Savannah in San Francisco

Gunner on the Coast

Michael at the Beach

Kris in the North Forests

Hope in Gold Country

Maddie in the Mojave Desert

Anna in Kings Canyon

Jennifer in Anza Borrego

Sarah & Gary at Lake Tahoe

Brett on the Coast

Lauren in Los Angeles

BEANIES IN THE WILD

Lisa at Olvera Street

Corina in the Northern Forests

Daniel in Gold Country

Elizabeth in Surf City

Lisa in Hollywood

Gary in Gold Country

Daniel in Sequoia

Donielle & Julie in Gold Country

Cheryl at Huntington Beach

Lisa in Los Angeles

Annabelle in Mojave Desert

Gary and Linda on the Coast

TECHNIQUES GLOSSARY

APPLYING/ PLACING BEADS

CROCHET HOOK METHOD

Using a crochet or bead hook appropriate for the size bead being used, insert the hook through the bead and leave the bead on the hook. With the crochet hook, pick up the loop of the stitch over which you want to place the bead and let it drop off your knitting needle. Pull this loop through the bead, place the loop back onto the left-hand needle, and remove the crochet hook. Knit this stitch in pattern to secure the bead.

STRINGING METHOD

Before any knitting begins, using a tapestry needle or sewing needle appropriate for the size bead being used, thread the needle with the tail of yarn for your project. Place all of the beads you plan to use onto the working needle, then pull them down the shaft of the needle and onto the working yarn. Move the beads down the yarn an appropriate length to allow you to cast on. Continue to move the beads down the yarn as you knit.

*To apply the bead, knit to your desired bead location. Then move the working yarn to the front of the work between the needles. Slide a bead along the working yarn until it is adjacent to the needle, in front of the work.

Slip the next stitch purlwise with the working yarn in front and slide the bead into place so that it nestles into the V of the slipped stitch.

Return the working yarn to the back between the needles and continue working in pattern.

Repeat from * until all beads are placed.

LONG-TAIL CAST-ON

Make a slipknot with the yarn, leaving a tail long enough to cast on the required number of stitches (usually about 1 in. / 2.5 cm per stitch), and place the slipknot onto the needle. Holding the needle in your right hand, clasp both strands for the cast on in the lower three fingers of your left hand with the long tail over your thumb and the end coming from the ball over your index finger.

*Spread your thumb and index finger apart to form a V. Insert the needle tip up between the two strands on your thumb. Bring the needle tip over the top of the first strand around your index finger, then down to draw a loop between the strands on your thumb. Remove your thumb and tighten the stitch on the needle—1 stitch cast on. Place your thumb and index finger between the strands of yarn again.

Repeat from * until the required number of stitches has been cast on.

DUPLICATE STITCH

Duplicate stitch is a way of adding sections of color to a knitted piece without having to work stranded knitting or intarsia. The technique covers each stitch completely. Large areas can become thick and stiff, so it's best used in small areas.

With the color to be stitched threaded into a tapestry needle, insert the needle from the wrong side to the right side in the stitch below the first stitch to be covered.

*Insert the tapestry needle under both legs of the stitch in the row above the stitch to be covered and pull the yarn through, being careful not to pull the yarn too tightly. Insert the needle back into the same spot where you initially brought it to the right side and pull the yarn through to completely cover the first stitch. Bring the needle up through the stitch below the next stitch to be covered.

Repeat from * to continue covering stitches.

FRENCH KNOT

The French knot is an embroidery method used to embellish your work by creating a decorative knot that is raised from the working surface. Thread a tapestry needle with a length of yarn approximately 12 in. / 30.5 cm long (for multiple knots; less length for a single knot).

Push the tapestry needle through the work from the wrong side to the right side (or back to front), leaving 2 in. /
5 cm of tail on the wrong side of the work for weaving in.

Holding the embroidery needle close to the surface of the work, wrap the working yarn around the tapestry needle as many times as indicated.

Using your pointer finger, hold the wraps against the tapestry needle and push the needle back through the work from the right side to the wrong side (or front to back) beside/near the original location (not into the same location to avoid the knot pulling through the work) and pull the yarn through the knot. Do not pull too snugly to avoid flattening the knot.

RESOURCES

NANCY BATES DESIGNS
www.nancybatesdesigns.com

Yarn

Note: If you don't immediately see the colors you need from the smaller scale indie dyers, be sure to send them a message.

ALY BEE WORKSHOP
www.alybeeworkshop.com

ANZULA LUXURY FIBERS
www.anzula.com

LANA GROSSA
www.lana-grossa.de/en/

LASER SHEEP YARNS
www.lasersheepyarns.com

LL YARN COMPANY
www.llyarnco.com

MALABRIGO
www.malabrigoyarn.com

PEEKABOO YARNS
www.etsy.com/shop/
PeekabooYarns

POLKA DOT SHEEP
www.polkadotsheep.com

STUNNING STRING STUDIO
www.stunningstring.com

URTH YARNS
www.urthyarns.com

WESTERN SKY KNITS
www.wsknits.com

ACKNOWLEDGMENTS

A world of gratitude and love goes to my husband, travel buddy, personal cheerleader, and Californian, Scott. I truly couldn't have done this without you!

To my wonderful daughters Natalie, Caitlin, and Alyson, thank you for the endless support, creative input, and FUN! Especially for all the road trip photo shoots both in front of and behind the camera. Who knew that raising you to love and appreciate the beauty of the state would someday end up helping me with such a creative project?

Much gratitude goes to test knitter, tech editor, and friend Sally Schultzman. Those biweekly meetups exchanging projects and ideas were more valuable than you know.

To long-distance test and sample knitter Donna Gober Raynor for happily taking on any project I needed, any time—many thanks!

It's impossible to design wearable knitted art without oodles of amazing yarn in incredible colors! Thank you, Alyson, Amy, and Tom for creating the beautiful colors I imagined, exactly when I needed them. Perfect!

A *huge* thanks to friend and fellow Canadian-turned-Californian, Barbara, for keeping my business going so I could focus on designing and writing. You're amazing!

Many thanks to my East Coast editor, Karyn, for your expertise, guidance, and especially your enthusiasm for learning about California! And to my publisher Roger for once again believing in an idea turning into a reality.

And...much love and appreciation to all of *YOU*, the knitters of my designs "in the wild" and around the world! ❤

MODEL AND PHOTOGRAPHY CREDITS

Thanks to all of the models who appear in this book:

Alyson Bates – 34, 46, 50, 58, 62, 72, 96, 100, 136, 140

Caitlin Bates – 4, 40, 66, 78

Natalie Bates – 2, 28, 76, 84, 88

Nancy Bates – 16, 20, 106, 110, 120, 122, 128, 132, 142, 160, 164, 172, 176, 179

Scott Bates – 90, 126, 178

Molly Conroy – 52, 56

Keri A. Dalebout – 116

Phoebe Graham – 103

Diane Hara – 13

Brigid Kumler – 22, 26

Mark Kumler – 94

Sally Schultzman – 166, 170

Neel Sutton – 154

Barbara Sweeney – 152

Jimmy Sweeney – 148

All beanie photography courtesy the Bates family.
All location photography is courtesy Shutterstock,
except for the following: Nancy Bates (p.104);
iStock (p.30 bottom); Photofest (p.30 top).

ABOUT THE AUTHOR

Nancy's love of color and texture and all things nature began at a very young age as she explored the hillsides in back of her neighborhood, sculpted elaborate mudpies in the yard, hand-sewed clothes for her Barbies, built "huts" with scraps of wood, and created art with whatever paint she could get her hands on. Over the years, embroidery, crochet, cross-stitch, and knitting were added to the list of creative endeavors that involved color and texture, most often inspired by the outdoors. The growing passion of combining knitting with a love of nature and home was the inspiration for her first book *Knitting the National Parks* and now *Knitting California*.

Since emigrating from Canada to California with her family at the age of two, Nancy has been exploring the state from her own neighborhood to the far reaches of nearly every corner for as long as she can remember, first with her parents and eight siblings and now with her own family. Today, she enjoys frequent weekend or week-long California getaways with her husband, inviting her three grown daughters and their growing families along as often as possible.

From her home in Southern California, Nancy operates her online business, visits yarn stores around the country whenever she travels, and enjoys teaching workshops about her signature embroidery on knitting techniques. You can find her on Instagram and Facebook where she encourages knitters to share stories and photos of their own knitting adventures.